Let's Make a Memory

Let's Make a Memory

Gloria Gaither & Shirley Dobson

GREAT IDEAS FOR BUILDING FAMILY
TRADITIONS AND TOGETHERNESS

Illustrated by RUSS FLINT

WORD PUBLISHING

Dallas • London • Vancouver • Melbourne

LET'S MAKE A MEMORY by Gloria Gaither and Shirley Dobson.
Copyright © 1983, 1994 by Gloria Gaither, Shirley Dobson, and James Dobson, Inc.

Scripture quotations marked KJV are from the King James Version of the Bible.

Scripture quotations marked NIV are from The Holy Bible: New International Version, copyright © 1973, 1978, 1984 by the New York International Bible Society, used by permission of Zondervan Bible Publishers.

Scripture quotations marked TLB are from *The Living Bible,* copyright 1971 by Tyndale House Publishers, Wheaton, Illinois. Used by permission.

Library of Congress Cataloging-in-Publications Data

Gaither, Gloria.
   Let's make a memory : great ideas for building family traditions and togetherness / Gloria Gaither and Shirley Dobson; illustrations by Russ Flint.
      p.   cm.
   "Rev. ed."
   ISBN 0-8499-3517-2
      1. Family—United States.   2. United States—Social life and customs.
   3. United States—Religious life and customs.   4. Holidays—United States.
   5. Creative activities and seatwork.
   I. Dobson Shirley 1937–   II. Flint Russ   III. Title.
   HQ536.G34   1994
   306.85'0973—dc20   94-30402
                                                                         CIP

Printed in the United States of America

4 5 6 7 8 9 0 DKN 9 8 7 6 5 4 3 2 1

*This book is
affectionately dedicated to
our husbands, Jim Dobson and Bill Gaither,
and to the Dobson children, Danae and Ryan, and
the Gaither children, Suzanne, Amy, and Benjy,
with whom we share lifetimes
of priceless memories.*

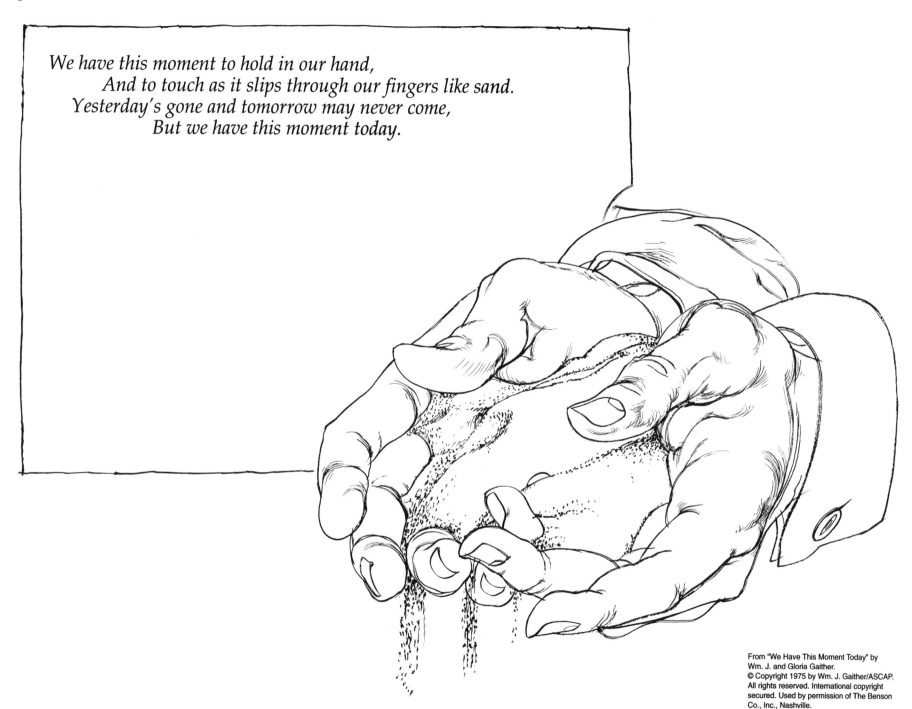

We have this moment to hold in our hand,
And to touch as it slips through our fingers like sand.
Yesterday's gone and tomorrow may never come,
But we have this moment today.

From "We Have This Moment Today" by
Wm. J. and Gloria Gaither.
© Copyright 1975 by Wm. J. Gaither/ASCAP.
All rights reserved. International copyright
secured. Used by permission of The Benson
Co., Inc., Nashville.

ACKNOWLEDGMENTS

Originality is the art of concealing your source, it is said, for there is no creative effort that does not draw on the inspiration we glean from one another. In this instance, however, we wish not to conceal—but to acknowledge—the sources that have contributed generously to the writing of this book. We are grateful to all who shared their family traditions with us, especially to those whose contributions appear in the Memorable Memory Makers section.

Also, we are indebted to others who encouraged and assisted us with the original version of the book in immeasurable ways, including:

Jan Starks, Flo Waltrip, Phyllis Esler, Dee Otte, and Helen Kolodny; Pat Wienandt, project managing editor; Beth Maybee, assistant editor; Merle Oliver, manuscript typist; Janice Gibson, finished art specialist; Dennis Hill, art director; Ronald Garman, project designer; and Russ Flint, illustrator. For this revised edition we also extend our thanks to Laura Kendall, project managing editor, and Tom Williams, art director.

These are the individuals for whom the greatest appreciation and love are due. But there is a larger body of contributors whom we *cannot* acknowledge personally. They represent the great host of unidentified conveyors of folk wisdom, crafts projects, and traditions that we've included in this book. We simply do not *know* where each of the ideas originated. They have become part of the culture in which we live. That is, in fact, the purpose for our book—to expand and vitalize those activities that give identity and meaning to the loving relationships within the context of today's families.

CONTENTS

GLORIA'S STORY

In my life I have been given many wonderful gifts: lovely handmade embroidered items, expensive works of art, earthy rustic crafts, primitive water paintings on simple newsprint created by the chubby little hands of children. I have been honored and complimented. I have had the thrill of hearing the songs I've helped to create recorded by famous singers and sung by congregations in my own and foreign languages. These are all gifts I treasure.

But none of these gifts has been so valuable to me as the gift of a rich childhood and youth in a solid, loving, celebrating home. The heritage of a family who loved God and each other, who greeted every new day with anticipation and openness, shaped my values and taught me that life was good. The healthy balance of discipline and freedom, the love of simple

things, the respect for all kinds of persons, a deep reverence for God—all these were wrapped up in special moments and given to me in the package I call my childhood.

I truly believe that most of what I've been able to do with my life has been a direct result of the rich heritage I enjoyed. I am certain that my family gave me a head start on life with a realistic concept of God and His Son, a love affair with nature, and an excitement for living. My home brought me to the threshold of adulthood with a secure confidence that I was loved and a deep responsibility to myself and the world around me for developing whatever special abilities and gifts God had given me.

My parents always pastored small Michigan churches, so we never traveled widely or were afforded the luxuries some families enjoy. Instead, we learned to celebrate life in simple ways and to create our own special moments and traditions from the raw material of common things. My mother, who was an artist and writer, taught my sister and me to see what many others missed. She gave us a deep appreciation for beauty and books and a great love for words and language. Daddy was the master of spur-of-the-moment parties on a shoestring: a Dairy Queen after church, a roadside picnic breakfast, the presentation of a special dress he'd scrimped to buy for Mother for an important event. It was Daddy who gave me my very own garden spot (even though he had to dig up the thick, green sod to do it) and gave me full rein to plant *anything* I wanted to. I learned from him the joy of "preferring one another," as every summer we would take fishing trips to the far north because Mother loved to fish. I remember him digging fishing worms, cleaning bass and catfish until midnight, lugging soggy rowboats into and out of the lakes, and rowing for miles, all just because he loved seeing Mother get so much fun out of "hooking a big one."

At our house everything was an event, and it was to our house that Evelyn's and my friends always came to "hang out"; we knew that if we needed a place for a gathering of any kind, it was okay to volunteer our place. Mother was the confidante for many a teenager, and it was not uncommon for someone in distress to knock on our door at midnight seeking comfort and advice. It never occurred to me to keep anything from her. She was my best friend. Soon our own children were running to her house whenever they needed someone to talk to or simply a place to be. She taught our son to paint with oils and to see things in the world around him that others miss. She critiqued our daughters' poetry and boyfriends. She was their best friend too.

When I married Bill, I found another big, loving family—an Indiana farm family, who loved the earth and celebrated harvests and holidays, Sundays and birthdays with big dinners and warm family gatherings: tables groaning with home-grown vegetables, fresh corn-fed meat, and steaming fruit desserts; children of all ages and sizes scampering around the patriarchs and assorted distant relations; the joyous noise of adult conversation, shrieking children, and spontaneous music.

Because we so appreciate our own heritages, Bill and I chose to live near both our families. We believed there was great value for our children in knowing their roots, which gave them a sense of perspective and continuity. In a society as mobile as the one we all live in, Bill and I feel very blessed that we were able to offer our children a close relationship with their extended family and close friendships with their young cousins and aging relatives. Living close to our extended family has not always been problem free, but we feel the benefits far outweigh any problems. Good or bad, family is family and life is life. We feel children need a realistic view of the influences that have come together to make up the sum total of what they are.

As Bill and I welcomed Suzanne, Amy, and Benjy into the world, we drew from the rich heritage we had been given to work toward becoming the kind of caring, compassionate family we believed God wanted us to be.

Now our children are establishing homes of their own, and Bill and I find great delight in watching them and their spouses pass on to our grandchildren the principles our parents gave us. We are all still "kids under construction," fed and nourished in the soil of our shared pasts from the seeds God has planted in us. Just as our parents contributed so much to our children's memory banks, we are now helping to make memories for our children's children!

So it was to celebrate the gift of our shared heritage that I worked with Shirley to create this book. Both of us, from our very different perspectives, believe that the family must be the basic spiritual, moral, educational, and physical unit of our society, or we will have no society.

We believe that special moments don't just *happen;* they have to be planned on *purpose!* In this hectic world when the pace at which we all live is so frantic, we as families must make a covenant with each other to make time for simple things. Please hear me now! *Special moments won't just happen.* Beautiful memories of yesterdays were once moments of todays. We have no guarantees of tomorrows, but we do have this moment.

The home is the natural habitat for growing human beings and shaping eternal souls. Whether we like it or not, we are molding lives . . . now. Let's make these precious moments count. Let's make a memory!

SHIRLEY'S STORY

I see a little girl skipping home from school in the late afternoon sun. Her dress is a hand-me-down, intended for someone two sizes larger. Her shoes are unpolished and her socks no longer have elastic around the top. She reaches her destination and walks across a barren yard toward a small house. It is badly in need of paint and repair, but the mother who lives there can barely afford to feed and clothe her son and daughter.

How tenderly I feel for this little child of poverty. It is almost as though she were my own daughter, and I ache to hold her in my arms . . . to buy her a pretty new dress . . . to give her a shiny new bicycle. But that is impossible—for we are separated by four decades of time. I can neither talk to her nor meet her needs. For that little girl, you see, is the memory of my own childhood. I walked in her shoes. I lived in that small unpainted house. And I can still feel the indescribable yearning of a child who knew that something vital was missing from her life.

I was the daughter of a confirmed alcoholic. Only those who have lived through this nightmare will understand the full implication of this experience. I could never ask a friend to spend the night for fear my father would return in a drunken stupor and embarrass me. Night after night, he would stumble home in the early morning hours, belligerent and foul-mouthed. We would be awakened by his shouting and threats and would often hide to avoid his wrath. The rooms of our home had been patched with brown butcher paper and painted over to conceal where he had shoved his fists through the walls in fits of anger.

Like other children of an alcoholic parent, I learned to hide my disgrace. I remember being driven home from a birthday party on one occasion and asking to be left at a clean house with a well-manicured yard. I waved good-bye and marched up the driveway as if it were my own, but when the car rounded the corner, I turned and walked several blocks to my house.

It was only through the wisdom and devotion of my mother that I survived the emotional pressures of those years. She is a strong woman, and she marshaled all of her resources to hold our little family together. Since Dad spent his entire paycheck at the bar each Friday night, Mother went to work to support the family. She found a job at a fish cannery which required her to work unpredictable hours. Many times she would be called at three or four in the morning after having been kept awake all night by her harassing, drunken husband. I marveled at her ability to hold a job and to do the marketing, cooking, housekeeping, and laundry under those stressful circumstances.

Most importantly, Mom convinced my brother and me that she loved us. And because of that love, she constantly sought ways to get us through those difficult years. She had the wisdom to know that she needed help in raising two rambunctious kids, and she turned for assistance to a local evangelical church. Mom would not go with us (Sunday was her "catch up" day), but she insisted that we get involved. She would pull back the blankets every Sunday morning and order us to get ready for church. We complained and moaned, but to no avail. Mom was not a practicing Christian, but she knew that churches offered more than one kind of "salvation," and her children needed all the help they could get.

It was in that little neighborhood church that I was introduced to Jesus Christ, and invited Him into my heart and life. He became my special friend, and I've never been the same since that moment. My pastor taught me that God cared about my personal concerns, so I began to pray for my

home. My father continued to drink and associate with other women, so our situation grew steadily worse. Finally, in desperation, I went into my bedroom and cried out to God:

> "If Dad isn't going to change, then please get us out of this house and give us the kind of father that will love and provide for us."

The Lord heard that prayer. After much suffering and agony involving Dad's continued drunkenness and an illicit relationship with a neighbor, my parents were divorced. I was in the sixth grade. We moved to a little shanty we called "our chicken coop," but for the first time, we could lie down in peace and enjoy an uninterrupted night's sleep.

My mother remarried a year later to a man who had been a confirmed bachelor. Joe was not a Christian at the time, but he was a man with high moral standards. We fell for his sunny disposition and big smile. He became a faithful husband and a good provider. Soon we moved to our first "real house," with bedrooms of our own and a front lawn with genuine grass and flowers. Later, both my mother and stepfather became beautiful Christians and remain committed to the faith today.

But there was another prayer that I sent toward heaven during those darkest days. As a ten-year-old girl, I began talking to God about the man I would eventually marry. I asked Him to send me a Christian husband when the time was right and not to let me fall into the private hell that my mother had experienced. Without realizing it, of course, I was praying at that moment for an eleven-year-old boy who was a thousand miles away, growing up in a loving, stable home like the one in my dreams.

My high school years proved to be relatively tranquil and I began to think about college. I enrolled in a Christian school with the financial help of my stepfather, and graduated four years later. Toward the end of my sophomore year, I began dating a tall, blond Texan named Jim Dobson. It didn't take me long to decide that he was the man I had been praying for since I was ten years old. I'll never forget the evening Jim and I were sitting in his car near the girls' dormitory, discussing our future together. He had asked me to marry him and I accepted. He turned to me and said, "I can't explain why you had to experience so much pain in your early childhood, but there is something I want you to know. I hereby pledge myself to the task of making up for those days. I am going to do the best I can to make you happy."

Jim and I soon will celebrate our thirty-fourth anniversary, and he has kept that youthful commitment. He has constructed my self-esteem as though he were a brick mason building a fortress. He has convinced me that I am a worthy person . . . that his love for me is unconditional, and that God has a place for me in His grand scheme for the universe. Our love for one another has never wavered throughout these three decades of daily togetherness, which is a miracle in itself. There is no doubt that God answered the second tearful prayer of a little girl named Shirley.

He also blessed us with two healthy, vibrant children and a lovely home. There are times when I stand and consider His gifts and find it difficult to realize that I am the recipient of them. Of course, to be honest, there have been difficult moments in our adult lives. We've experienced our share of reverses and sad times and illnesses. During one three-year period, for example, we lost eight members of our small family in death.

But even during these times of tragedy, the presence of God has been evident to each of us. We will, after all, be united on the other side.

As I look back on the painful experience of my childhood, I am overwhelmed with gratitude to God for answering my early prayers. He heard the desperate cries of a ten-year-old girl who could offer Him nothing in return. I had no status, no special abilities, no money to contribute. My father was not a physician or a lawyer or a member of the city council. I was totally without dignity or social influence. Yet the Creator of the universe entered my little room and communed with me about the difficulties I was experiencing. It was awesome to realize that He loved me just as I was, and my pain became His pain. What a magnificent God we serve!

Is there any wonder why I believe literally in the Scripture that promises, "Trust in the Lord with all thine heart and lean not unto thine own understanding. In all thy ways acknowledge Him, and He shall direct thy paths" (Prov. 3:5–6 KJV)?

I have provided this background to explain why the topic for our book has become so important to me. My early home, by necessity, had no traditions whatsoever. At Christmas time, for example, we never knew if we would be able to afford a tree or gifts to put under it. There was no special dinner or even any forethought for the holidays. Yuletide was just another financial hurdle to be scaled.

But when I married into the Dobson family, I saw the glorious meaning of loving interdependency throughout the year. The Dobsons are a proud southern family steeped in tradition. Many of their annual festivals are centered around customary meals. My husband, Jim, says, "The great value of traditions comes as they give a family a sense of identity, a belongingness. All of us desperately need to feel that we're not just a cluster of people living together in a house, but we're a family that's conscious of its uniqueness, its personality, character and heritage, and that our special relationships of love and companionship make us a unit with identity and personality."

These words contain great wisdom for meaningful family life, and we are attempting to implement them in our home. In fact, the purpose for this book is to help you establish similar traditions in your home. Gloria and I have prepared a "how to" book that we hope will enrich the lives of your children and loved ones.

Today is the last day of your past and the first day of your future. There's no better time than now to begin "making memories" with your precious family.

MAKING MEMORABLE HOLIDAYS / SPECIAL DAYS

THIS DAY

There is beauty in the morning
With the sun tip-toeing in,
When the day's a brand new conscience
And the world's a chance to win.

There is muscle in the noontime
When the sun is plowing through
Hot and bright and clear and brawny,
Nature's time to go and do.

There's a charm about the evening—
Gentle, loving like a friend,
Smiling o'er the west horizon,
Tying up the day's loose ends.

Lovely, complicated wrappings
Sheath the gift of one-day-more;
Breathless, I untie the package—
Never lived <u>this</u> day before!

Gloria Gaither

From *Rainbows Live at Easter*
Copyright © 1974 by Gloria Gaither

ON NEW YEAR'S EVE

A TIME TO REFLECT

- On New Year's Eve, give each family member an unlighted candle.

- Lower the lights and select one person to be the "candle lighter."

- As each family member's candle is lighted, have him or her make one request of God for the coming year: help in meeting a new goal, maintaining a priority, working on a better relationship with another family member, or other similar requests.

- Close with a prayer of thanksgiving for God's provision and protection during the past year.

- Serve a traditional snack—soup and a cheese tray, or other favorite combination.

CHAMP FOR THE YEAR

- On New Year's Eve, while waiting for midnight, choose a family game that all can play—Yahtzee, Sorry, Monopoly, or other favorite.

- Record the winner for the coming year in the lid of the box. Over the years it will be fun to see who reigned as the New Year's "champ" from one December 31 to the next December 31.

HAPPY NEW YEAR

FAMILY DIARY

- Begin a "family diary" on the first day of the new year.

- Take turns writing about events and activities that occur on each day or week throughout the year.

- At the end of the year, schedule an evening to review and discuss the happenings of the previous twelve months.

CHILD'S SPECIAL WEEKEND

- At the beginning of the new year, designate one weekend during the coming twelve months for each child and write those dates on the master calendar.

- Let each child choose the activities he or she prefers on his or her special weekend, such as backpacking, fishing, bicycling, skating, visiting the zoo, or other practical possibility.

- When the children are grown, they should have a storehouse of special memories that were built during these family weekend experiences.

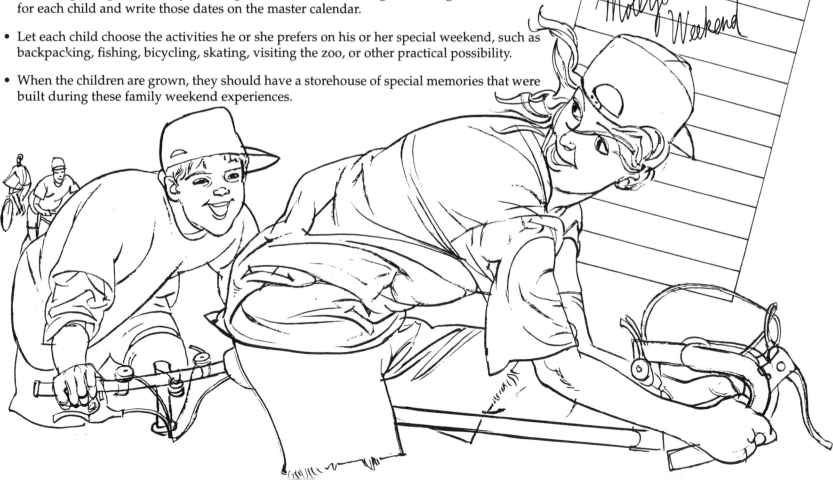

FAMILY FUN THROUGHOUT THE YEAR

MATERIALS NEEDED

Decorated coffee can
Colored construction paper
3" x 3" cardboard patterns,
   one for each family member
Scissors
Pencils

- During the first week of the New Year, place a colorfully decorated coffee can near the kitchen table. Label it "Family Fun Throughout the Year."

- Give each member of the family a different colored piece of construction paper, scissors, pencils, and a 3" x 3" cardboard pattern.

- Trace the square pattern five times on the construction paper and cut out the squares.

- Have each person write on each of their squares a family activity he or she would like to do on "Family Fun" night. Then drop the slips of paper in the container.

- Each week, draw one activity from the can. The person whose color was selected one week does not get another turn until all the other colors have been chosen. This method gives every individual a turn to choose an activity and adds mystery and excitement to the evening.

- Replenish the coffee can with new cards when all the suggestions have been implemented.

HOMEMADE VALENTINES

Make your own valentines for family members. The handmade ones are still the best.

MATERIALS NEEDED

White and red construction paper
Lace, bits of ribbon or yarn, paper doilies, or other decorative materials
White glue
Crayons or markers
Old magazines

- Cut an 8 ½" x 11" sheet of construction paper in half.

- Fold each half double (each full sheet will make two cards).

- Decorate the cover with hearts, pictures, lace, doilies, ribbons, etc.

- Compose a poem or verse for your loved one, or write a short essay on "This Is What You Mean to Me" or "You're Something Special Because . . ."

- Copy the poem inside the card.

- Envelopes to fit this size card can be purchased at stationery, computer, and office-supply stores or can be made by hand.

BELOVED SILHOUETTES

MATERIALS NEEDED

Slide projector, spotlight,
   or other bright light source
Poster board
Pencil
Red construction paper
Broad-tipped felt pen or marker
Scissors
Paper doilies (optional)

- Use a slide projector, Viewmaster, or spotlight to project the head profile silhouette of each person in the family onto a blank wall. A bright lamp with the shade removed also provides a good light source.

- Hold poster board against the wall and trace the silhouette with a pencil. Go over the pencil lines with a broad-tipped pen or marker.

- Cut out each silhouette.

- Cut a heart shape from a sheet of red construction paper or poster board larger than the size of the silhouette.

- Paste each silhouette on a separate heart and display them along a hallway or send them to grandparents for valentines.

HINT: A heart-shaped paper doily may be pasted under the silhouette, using contrasting colors. For instance, use a red heart with a white doily placed on it. Then paste the red or black silhouette on top of the doily.

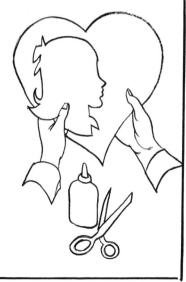

SPECIAL DAYS / VALENTINE'S DAY

VALENTINE TREASURE HUNT

- Buy a package of inexpensive children's valentines.

- Write a different love note on each of ten to fifteen cards; or write one word per card to form a message of love.

- Hide the cards throughout the house, in the car, or in other suitable places.

- Give a written clue on the outside of each envelope directing your "valentine" to the next card.

- Include a small "love gift" with the last valentine.

VALENTINE NOTES

LOVE GIFT MESSAGES

- Write love notes to each member of your family, telling why you love and appreciate him or her. Be specific!

- Tuck the notes in lunch boxes, notebooks, or briefcases along with a special valentine treat.

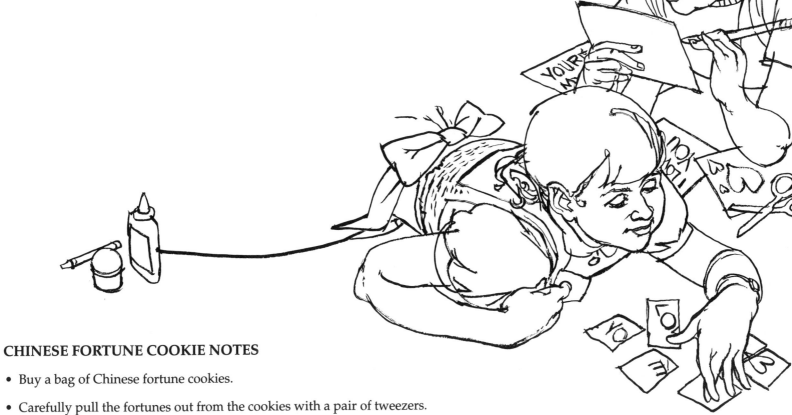

CHINESE FORTUNE COOKIE NOTES

- Buy a bag of Chinese fortune cookies.

- Carefully pull the fortunes out from the cookies with a pair of tweezers.

- Cut up small slips of paper and write your own messages of love in one sentence, roll them up, and slip them back into the fortune cookies. Or write your messages on several pieces of paper that must be fitted together like a puzzle. The messages can also be clever or funny if the occasion dictates.

SPECIAL DAYS / VALENTINE'S DAY

HOW MOM AND DAD MET

- With the family gathered around, have Dad and Mom tell the story of their first date and their courtship. They may include:

  – how and where they met.
  – activities and places they enjoyed while dating.
  – when they fell in love.
  – what qualities attracted them to one another.
  – how Dad proposed.
  – humorous stories about their courtship.

- Have Dad and Mom show old pictures of themselves when they were young.

- As a nice touch, Dad might even show the family how he kissed Mom the very first time!

PASSOVER (BACKGROUND)

God commanded in Exodus 12 that this day be kept. Passover is the celebration of God's delivering His people out of the slavery of Pharaoh. The word *passover* refers to the night of the worst plague God sent to Egypt because Pharaoh, the Egyptian ruler, would not let the people go free. (Read about the plagues in Exodus 9–12, preferably from *The Living Bible*.)

On that night, God promised that He would visit every house to execute judgment and would take the life of the firstborn son unless the family had marked the door of their house with the blood of a perfect lamb. If a family obeyed God and marked their doors, He would "pass over" that house and no one in that family would die.

This plague finally convinced Pharaoh to let God's people go. Even to this day, Jewish families and many Christian families celebrate the feast of Passover, as God instructed. Jesus and His disciples were Israelites, and it was this celebration that He shared with His disciples at His last supper with them.

All Christians celebrate Communion—the breaking of bread and sharing of the cup of wine—because Jesus instructed His followers to remember Him in this way.

The father or grandfather is seated at the head of the table. The dishes to be served should be where the father can pass them to the family.

As the meal progresses, the youngest son asks the father or grandfather the following question four different times: "Why is this night different from all other nights?"

The first time the son asks the question, the father answers as he serves the unleavened bread: "For on other nights we eat bread, but tonight we eat

only *matzoth*." Then he explains the meaning of this bread.

The second time, the father answers: "For on other nights we eat other vegetables, but tonight we eat only bitter herbs." He serves the *maror* and then explains the reason.

The third time, the father answers the son's question this way: "For on other nights we do not dip our vegetables even once; but tonight—we dip twice." Salt water is then passed and the father explains that it represents tears of sorrow. The parsley represents the new life, but we dip it in salt water to remind us of the tears and the sacrifice that was made to make springtime and new life possible. Next, we dip the bitter herbs in *haroseth,* which sweetens the bitterness of the herbs and reminds us that the sacrifice was sweetened by freedom. The color of the *haroseth* reminds us of the mortar the Hebrew slaves had to use to erect buildings for their masters.

A fourth time the youngest son asks the ritual question, to which his father answers: "For all other nights we eat sitting up, but tonight we all recline." Then he explains that in the old days free men sat on soft chairs or on couches, but servants had to stand before their masters or, while eating, sit on a hard bench. "Tonight, we celebrate our deliverance and freedom, so we sit in comfort and enjoy our freedom, wishing the same for all people."

This meal should end for Christians with the explanation that we are all "chosen people" if we have been "born" into God's family by believing in His Son, Jesus, as our Messiah. As God's people, then, we should share the cup of joy with others out of gratitude that Jesus became the final "Lamb" to be sacrificed in order that "our joy may be full."

THE PASSOVER SEDER (SUPPER)

Passover lasts seven or eight days and begins with a meal and worship service Jewish families call Seder, or "order," because they always keep the celebration in a certain order. This first meal is made up of specific foods. Each has a special meaning.

To celebrate Seder you would serve:

- *Matzoth*—wafers of unleavened bread. (Can be secured from a Jewish delicatessen or from some grocers.) This is to remind us of the fact that the Israelites did not have time to wait for yeast bread to rise because they had to be ready to move when God said. For Christians, this reminds us also to live so that we are always "ready to go" when Jesus returns. Also, yeast sometimes represented the evil in the world. God wants His people to be pure.

- *Maror*—bitter herbs, usually freshly grated horseradish or other bitter, pungent vegetable such as onion. These herbs are a reminder of the bitter suffering in Egyptian slavery. This also reminds us that many have suffered that we may know the joy of the good news of Jesus. So in our celebration, we remember the great cost.

- *Haroseth*—a mixture of chopped apples, nuts, cinnamon, and wine. This represents the mortar with which the Israelites were forced to make bricks to build Pharaoh's great cities. (See Exodus 2:11–14 and 5:4–23.)

- *The shank bone of a lamb.* This is a symbol of the lamb that was sacrificed for sins. To Christians, this represents Jesus, God's own gift of a perfect Lamb for the sins of all.

- *A roasted egg*—an egg hard-boiled in the shell. Symbol of the free-will offering that was given with the lamb. This represents giving more to God than just what is demanded. This is a gift of love. Jesus was God's ultimate gift. God's law demanded only justice, but with the gift of Jesus, God gave us more than justice; He gave us mercy, love, and forgiveness.

- *Parsley or watercress.* These two plants stay green the year around and represent the continual rebirth of growing things. To Christians, this represents God's gift of everlasting life because of the Resurrection.

- *Wine or grape juice.* Wine represents joy. As the service proceeds, as each plague is mentioned, each person sips a little of the wine. This means that until total liberation, joy was incomplete. Jesus said at the Last Supper that the wine represented His own life's blood, poured out for us. He meant that He had to die so that we could know the total joy of freedom and forgiveness.

- *Elijah's cup.* In the center of the table is placed a goblet of wine or grape juice that represents Elijah, whom the Israelites believed would foretell the coming of the Messiah.

This cup remains full to welcome Elijah and his announcement of the Messiah's return. Christians believe that John the Baptist was this "Elijah." Jesus said in Matthew 11:14 that if the people could understand what was happening, they would recognize John as the promised Elijah who was to announce the Messiah's coming. For Christians, this cup does not remain untouched, but is shared by everyone at the table in the joy that our hope has come true. The Messiah has come to us and is alive to give our lives eternal joy.

SPECIAL DAYS / PASSOVER

SYMBOLS OF EASTER

Many times we enjoy the symbols of a special day without really understanding what they mean. Easter symbols are especially meaningful. Before Easter we might discuss the messages of these tokens we so enjoy.

- *Spring.* Easter and spring belong together. What a wonderful time to celebrate newness of life and the resurrection when all nature is "rising again."

- *Baby bunnies, chicks, birds.* All newly born creatures remind us of the new birth in Christ. Because of Easter we can become "new creatures" in Him.

- The *green, yellow, pink,* and *lavender* colors of springtime. These are perfect to symbolize Easter. Earth bursts forth into color with the proclamation "Life wins!" Green also stands for new life, and lavender, the color of royalty, reminds us that Jesus is King of Kings and Lord of Lords.

- *New clothes.* A new outfit symbolizes the putting away of winter—the time when it seems all nature hides "in the tomb"—and the dressing up of the earth in the lovely new clothes of summer. We, too, because of Christ's bursting from the tomb, are "clothed in newness of life."

- *Eggs.* Eggs, of course, are the epitome of promised life—life sealed away for a time before new life literally bursts forth! Eggs also symbolize in Jewish tradition a free-will offering, the giving of more than is demanded. Jesus is God's free-will offering. God gives us far beyond what we deserve or even dare to ask. Jesus is the gift not only of life, but of eternal life!

"JESUS IS RISEN"

Children *love* to decorate hard-boiled eggs.

- Try writing messages on the eggs with crayons before dyeing to remind you of the real meaning of Easter. Examples of messages are:

  "Jesus Loves You"

  "Love—Forever"

  "Jesus Died For You"

  "Born Again"

  "He Is Risen"

  "Love Changes Things"

  "Hallelujah"

EASTER MOSAICS

MATERIALS NEEDED

Large sheet of poster board
Old crayons, assorted colors
Glue

- Trace or draw a simple Easter picture onto a piece of poster board.

- Remove all paper from old crayons.

- Cut crayons into pieces $\frac{1}{4}$- to $\frac{1}{2}$-inch long.

- Stand crayon pieces on end and glue them to picture, filling areas in solid with colors to match those in picture.

- Display your crayon mosaic.

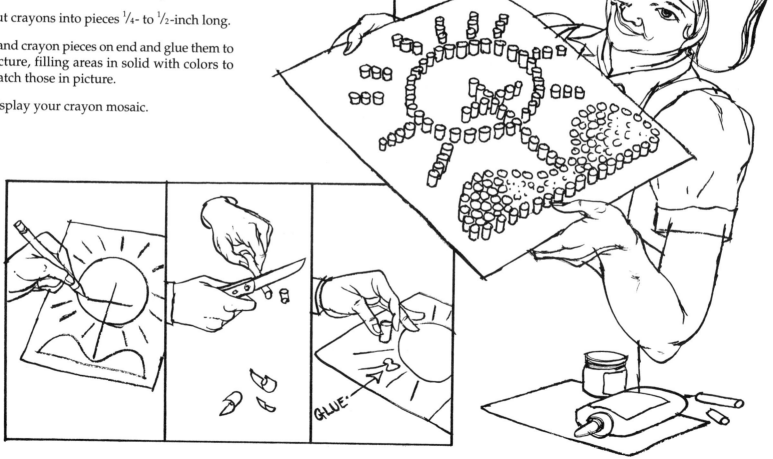

EASTER SATURDAY

- Celebrate the children's "fun" part of Easter on Saturday, reserving Sunday for worship and reflection on the death and resurrection of Jesus.

- Hide eggs and Easter baskets on Saturday, including a special "treasure egg."

- Buy or make a large plastic or papier-mâché egg. Enclose a small "treasure" inside the egg such as money, a gift, a candy treat, or a small toy.

- Hide the special egg carefully. It is best for the children to find the other eggs before locating the "treasure egg." This increases the suspense and competition as children search for the "hidden treasure."

- Decorate your table with an Easter theme, and serve refreshments after the hunt.

SPECIAL DAYS / EASTER

FAMILY EASTER EGG HUNT

- Fill plastic eggs with small "treasures" such as candy, coins, or tiny gifts. If you have small children, be careful to choose candies and toys that aren't likely to cause choking. Real eggs may be hard-boiled and colored if desired.

- Hide all eggs ahead of time.

- Talk about why eggs can be symbols of Easter, for example, to represent the promise of new life that the tomb held for us all.

- Give each person (grown-ups, too) a paper lunch sack decorated with an Easter sticker.

- Begin the hunt with a starting signal.

- After about ten to fifteen minutes, blow a whistle, calling everyone in.

- Take turns showing each other the treasures found.

- Pass out prizes to everyone, or celebrate with Easter cake and milk or other beverage.

FAMILY COMMUNION

AHEAD OF TIME

- Read about Passover and what it meant from a Bible storybook or from the Bible (see Exodus 12).

- Explain why the Jewish families ate unleavened bread when they remembered Passover (see page 25).

- Read passages leading up to the account of The Last Supper (John 13), Jesus' last words to His disciples (John 14–16), and Jesus' prayer for us (John 17).

- Explain that Jesus became the Passover Lamb as a sacrifice for our sins forever.

- Discuss what it means to share His cup (John 18:11).

- Discuss what it means to be part of the body of Christ.

- Be sure the children understand and participate with reverence.

SHARING THE ELEMENTS OF THE FAMILY COMMUNION

- Use one loaf of unleavened bread and one cup so that the family may share "One Body" and "One Cup." (If it is your conviction that only a clergyperson must administer Communion, invite your pastor to do so in the circle of your family.)

- It is meaningful to share with each person with whom you break bread why you feel that person has been a gift from God to you. Jesus said "I love you" with a cross. We need to practice freely saying it to each other.

- Thank God together for the gift of His Son, for forgiveness, and for adopting each of us into His own family, making us sons and daughters of God and brothers and sisters with the Lord Jesus, who brought us to the Father with His own life.

FAMILY SUNRISE SERVICE

AHEAD OF TIME

- Choose a special, quiet place from which the sunrise can be seen.

- Prepare a simple, carry-along breakfast of boiled eggs, rolls, juice, etc. (If you like, each person's breakfast could be packed in a colorful Easter basket. Surprises could be hidden in the bottom of each basket.)

- Find and mark the Easter story in the Bible.

- Choose one or two songs the whole family can sing about the risen Lord, or take along a cassette player and taped music the family can sing along with.

- The week before Easter, read from a Bible storybook or from the Bible about the events leading up to the Resurrection (Matthew 26, 27) and discuss them.

- The night before Easter, talk about how the disciples must have felt on the Saturday night before the Resurrection; how Jesus' mother must have felt; what Mary Magdalene and those who had known Jesus were feeling.

EASTER MORNING

- Rise early enough to give the family time to get to your special place just before the sun comes up.

- Wear clothes that can be gotten into quickly (you can get ready for church later). Take warm jackets and blankets.

- Spread a blanket to sit on; then read together about the women going to Jesus' tomb and what they experienced.

- As the sun comes peeping over the horizon, sing or play a victorious song. Then thank God *with your eyes wide open* for the Resurrection and what it means to your family.

- Celebrate by sharing the simple breakfast you have brought with you.

TRADITIONAL EASTER BRUNCH

Plan your own traditional brunch. Serve the same foods each year. A sample menu might include: orange juice, fresh fruit, scrambled eggs, and apple muffins.

The recipe provided here is a Dobson favorite. It was given to Shirley by a dear friend whose mother made apple muffins every Saturday morning.

EASTER APPLE MUFFINS

1 cup chopped apples (apples should be pared and thinly sliced, $1/4$-in., before chopping)
$1/4$ cup sugar
1 egg (well-beaten)
$2/3$ cup milk
$1/4$ cup butter

•

2 cups flour
$1/2$ tsp. salt
$1/2$ tsp. cinnamon
$1/4$ cup sugar
4 tsp. baking powder

TOPPING:

4 tbsp. melted butter
2 tbsp. sugar
1 tsp. cinnamon

In large bowl mix together apples and $1/4$ cup sugar. Blend in egg. Add milk and butter and mix together lightly. Sift in dry ingredients: flour, salt, cinnamon, sugar, and baking powder. Mix together well. Spoon into greased or paper-lined muffin tins. In a separate bowl mix together topping. Add topping to each muffin. Bake at 350 degrees for 20 minutes. Serves 12.

RESURRECTION BUNS

1 package of Rhodes frozen bread dough rolls
24 large marshmallows
melted butter or margarine
sugar mixed with cinnamon

Thaw 24 rolls. Flatten a roll to about 3" in diameter. Place a large marshmallow in the center of dough and pinch the dough together around the marshmallows. Roll in the palm of your hands and smooth into a softball sized dough ball. Roll in butter, roll in cinnamon and sugar, place on a greased cookie sheet. Let them rise until they double in size (30–60 min.) Bake at 350 degrees for 15–20 minutes until golden brown. Remove from pan and cool on a wire rack. Just like the tomb on Easter Sunday these buns are empty! Enjoy!

JULY 4 PATRIOT PARADE

AHEAD OF TIME

- Send or call invitations to family and friends to join in the parade.

- Decorate everything that has wheels (bikes, trikes, wagons, "Big Wheels," doll buggies) with red, white, or blue paper stars, crepe-paper streamers, ribbons, etc. Rollerskaters, rollerbladers, or skateboarders could wear patriotic costumes.

- Have each person who is going to be in the parade choose a patriot to represent. Collect or make suitable costumes from crepe paper, construction paper, and grown-ups' old clothes. Some possible characters: George Washington, Betsy Ross, Uncle Sam, Abraham Lincoln, Daniel Boone, Davy Crockett, Paul Revere, Martha Washington, a bugler, a drummer.

- Get the family pets into the act by tying bright red, white, or blue ribbons, bows, or strips of paper to leashes, collars, cages, or pet boxes—even fishbowls.

NOTE: Be careful not to put pets close together if they don't like each other (or if they like each other too well).

AT THE SCHEDULED TIME

- Have those not in the parade sit in lawn chairs where they can see the "parade route."

- Announce the beginning of the parade with a bugle call, after which the drummer(s) lead off the procession.

- Have the announcer introduce each patriot or parade entry as that "act" goes by the stands.

- After the parade, have the announcer invite everyone to join in singing "America the Beautiful."

- Serve everyone juicy cold slices of watermelon.

- With adult supervision, sparklers or other fireworks can be added as a finale in areas where they are allowed.

UNSCRAMBLE THE CODE*

- Select an appropriate Bible verse; for example, Chronicles 7:14.

- Write it on a piece of paper in the following code form:

  IEFEMEYEPEEEOEPELEEEWEHEIECE
  HEAEREEECEAELELEEEDEBEYEMEYE
  NEAEMEEESEHEAELELE . . . etc.

- Give the family several minutes to decipher the code.

- If the code is still unsolved after ten minutes, give clues as necessary, waiting two or three minutes after each clue before giving the next one. Such clues could be:

  1. The letter "E" separates the letters and the words.
  2. Look up 2 Chronicles 7:14.

- Have each family member write down the words. When everyone has finished, quote the verse together.

- Allow some time to memorize the verse. See who can memorize it first.

- Discuss how the Scripture applies to America. Ask relevant questions: Is God forgotten in our country? How? Is He honored? How?

* Appreciation is expressed to *Family Life Today* for use of this idea.

SPECIAL DAYS / PATRIOTIC DAYS

PATRIOTIC GIFTS

A PRESENT FOR OUR LAND

- Plan to give a living and growing present to our land. Planting a tree or bush would be a great family project.

- Discuss what kind of plant should be selected and where it would grow best.

- Talk about the positive reasons for giving such a gift: it releases oxygen into the atmosphere; it gives shelter to the birds; it provides beauty and shade, etc.

- Plant the tree or bush in your own yard, or ask the city or park services to select an appropriate spot for it in the community.

- Plan how to care for your plant.

JULY 4 "WE LOVE YOU AMERICA" DINNER

- Plan an all-American dinner including such traditional foods as hot dogs, hamburgers, apple pie, ice cream, etc.

- Decorate the table with a patriotic theme, using red, white, and blue napkins, tablecloth, flowers, etc.

- If a globe is available, point out the United States to the young children. Talk about the countries that surround it, the customs of the people, and reasons people love the countries they live in.

- Look in the encyclopedia for the article discussing this special holiday and read it aloud.

- Discuss the article as a family. Ask each child to recite one important fact or idea he or she learned.

- This dinner can be served on other patriotic days besides July 4: Memorial Day, Flag Day, Veterans Day, Washington's or Lincoln's birthday, etc.

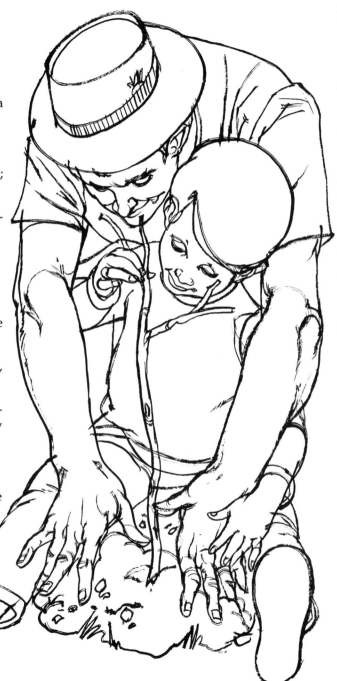

HAPPY BIRTHDAY AMERICA CAKE

- Let the children help bake a cake in celebration of Independence Day (or other patriotic day). It can be a round cake topped with red, white, and blue candles and small American flags, a 9" x 13" rectangular cake decorated with a flag design, or other appropriate shape or design.

- Sing "Happy Birthday, America"; then cut the cake and enjoy.

- Serve red punch with blue ice cubes (tinted with food coloring). Drink fast before the ice melts!

- Have Dad tell the story of how our country was founded and the meaning of the Declaration of Independence (or significant fact about the patriotic day that is being celebrated).

- In areas where fireworks are not illegal, enjoy them together after the sun has gone down. *Adult supervision is a MUST.* Or enjoy a fireworks show put on by your city or other local group.

SPECIAL DAYS / PATRIOTIC DAYS

SPECIAL DAYS / LABOR DAY

WORK

GOD'S PERFECT PLAN

Work was always a part of God's plan. The first thing God gave to Adam was a job: to name all living things, and "to dress" and "to keep" the garden. Work was a gift and was intended to be a joy.

Make banners to put up in your house to celebrate God's plan for work. Here are some suggestions:

- "The firmament showeth His handiwork." (Ps. 19:1 KJV)

- "We must do the work of him who sent me." (John 9:4 NIV)

- "We are labourers together with God." (1 Cor. 3:9 KJV)

- "The people had a mind to work." (Neh. 4:6 KJV)

- "Be strong . . . and work: for I am with you." (Hag. 2:4 KJV)

- "He is the Rock, his work is perfect." (Deut. 32:4 KJV)

- "[Be] a workman who does not need to be ashamed." (2 Tim. 2:15 NIV)

THE GIFT OF WORK

To help your children appreciate the gift of work, make arrangements ahead of time to take them to your place of employment on a regular work day, or if that is impossible, collect materials, pictures, or artifacts that will demonstrate the work you do.

- Begin the day by talking about the gift that work is to our lives and the joy we find in contributing to other persons' lives through our skills.

- Take an outing to your place of employment. (If both parents work, include both places of employment.)

- Show the facility, your special place of work, and introduce the children to some of the persons with whom you work.

- Let the children learn about the end result of your specific job. You may want to eat together in the plant cafeteria, office snack shop, or nearby restaurant where you often go for lunch. If you take your lunch, pack a lunch for each person in the family and eat together at your usual place.

- At the end of the day, discuss the jobs each person in the family does to make the home run smoothly. Thank God for the health, strength, and intelligence to work.

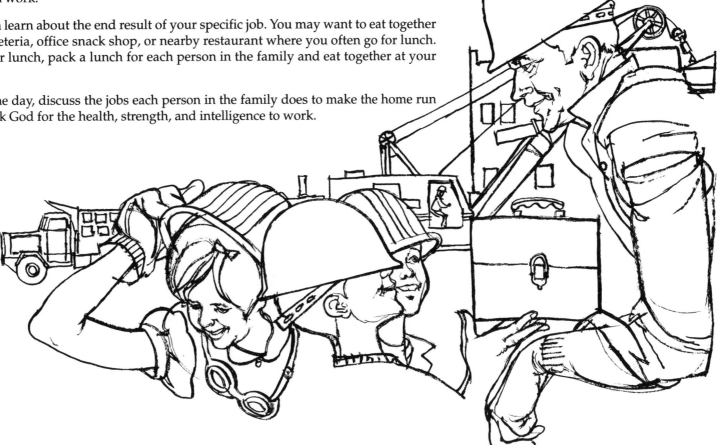

GREAT QUOTES

A lot has been said about work. Make a collection of great quotes about work and type or print the ones you like the best on strips of colored paper. Or make a unique design for your quote using computer graphic software. Tack them in random design on a family bulletin board or tape them to doors about the house. See the illustration for suggestions.

At supper on Labor Day, require, as the admission fee to the supper table, the recitation of one memorized quote about work.

MY FAMILY'S WORK HERITAGE

Make a game of a family research project. See who can find out the most about what your ancestors did for their life's work.

- Buy each family member a spiral notebook for keeping notes and compiling "work profiles."

- Use a cassette recorder or video camera to "document" bits of interesting information.

POSSIBLE SOURCES OF INFORMATION

- Interview older family members and ask information about the types of work skills of members of your family tree.

- Find your family's genealogy (most families have one member who is interested in completing this document) and read to find interesting occupations. Old family Bibles often give information about what family members did for a living.

- Make a list of the most famous and infamous "workers" in your family's history.

- Make a list of times in history when the need for work changed the course of family history.

- Make a list of what the young people in your family think they might like to do as their life's work.

- List vocations that are available today that did not exist two generations ago.

- Thank God for the wide opportunity for work available to us today. Thank Him for each person's specialness and the chance to express that uniqueness in the work we do.

SPECIAL DAYS / LABOR DAY

FAMILY PUMPKIN ART

AHEAD OF TIME

Find out about places in your area where pumpkins are grown and make arrangements to visit one with your family during the peak of harvest. If there is no such place, begin in early spring to grow your own pumpkins. Consult a gardener for instructions for your locale that will produce some fine pumpkins by October.

- Make a family outing of the pumpkin-finding hunt, allowing each person (parents, too) to choose one pumpkin.

- If apple cider is available at the pumpkin farm, have a glass of it together, or take a gallon of cider home to enjoy later.

- When you arrive home, if the weather permits, spread several layers of newspaper on the driveway before beginning work on the pumpkins. (You may have to work inside the house or in the garage.)

- Carve or draw faces on the pumpkins, each person creating his/her own masterpiece. If there are young children, felt-tip markers should be used instead of knives.

- If pumpkins are carved (save some seeds to roast), put a candle inside each one to illuminate your artwork (a little melted wax will keep the candle upright).

- Display the carved-pumpkin masterpieces on your porch or sidewalk.

- After supper, as it gets dark, make some hot spiced cider and pop some corn. (See recipe for hot cider on page 110.)

- Have one grown-up or older child light the candles, then go out together to see the glowing results.

- Serve everyone some hot cider and popcorn.

RECIPE FOR ROASTED PUMPKIN SEEDS

- Obtain a fresh pumpkin.

- Cut into the pumpkin and separate seeds from pulp.

- Wash seeds in a colander.

- Drain them on several layers of paper towel.

- In a large skillet, melt 2 tbsp. margarine (butter scorches more easily). Add 1 tsp. salt.

- Add 2 cups pumpkin seeds and saute about 3 minutes, stirring so that all seeds are coated with margarine.

- Place seeds on a cookie sheet and bake for about 25 minutes in an oven preheated to 300 degrees.

- Drain on a paper towel until pumpkin seeds are crisp and cool enough to eat.

FALL FAUX FACES

- Decorate for this party with harvest grains, nuts, fruits, vegetables (apples, gourds, and pumpkins, etc.), and colorful leaves.

- Set a harvest-time atmosphere with warm lighting effects and music.

- Let the children dress up in their costumes and masks. Discuss the characters they are pretending to be. They might choose a Christian theme using Bible characters, or nursery rhymes, or cartoon characters.

- Talk about the different kinds of invisible masks we sometimes wear. Why do we wear them?

- Let each member of the family share some of their fears—real or imaginary. Discuss how these might be diminished or dispelled.

- For refreshments, serve orange soda and cupcakes decorated with candy leaves or candy corn.

DESIGN-YOUR-OWN MASQUERADE COSTUME

- Obtain a piece of wrapping paper equal in length to your child's height.

- A week or more before the masquerade party, have your small child lie down on the piece of wrapping paper, and trace around him or her with a broad-tipped pen or marker.

- Cut out the shape you have traced.

- Let the child draw directly onto the shape with crayons the design of the costume he or she would like.

- Mom will then try to make (or put together from available clothes and materials) a costume according to the design the child has created.

THANKSGIVING AT THE DOBSONS . . .

Thanksgiving is given major prominence in the Dobson home. It marks the beginning of the holiday season and the happy gathering with relatives who live close by. When the day arrives, excitement and anticipation fill the air. Wonderful mouth-watering aromas of turkey, dressing, and apple pies float from the kitchen as family members arrive. A new jigsaw puzzle is placed on the card table with a pot of hot coffee nearby. Various lawn games are set up in the backyard and a spirited basketball game is soon organized on the driveway.

When dinnertime is announced, we gather around the table and Jim reads a Scripture. Everyone takes the hand of the person sitting next to him or her and Jim prays a prayer of thankfulness to God. After the traditional meal has been eaten and the table is cleared for dessert, two kernels of dried Indian corn are placed beside each plate. I explain that this represents the first Thanksgiving when the Pilgrims came to America and endured such a difficult winter and how grateful they were to God for bringing them through. A little basket is then passed around and as each kernel is dropped into the basket, we describe two blessings for which we are most thankful. The comments invariably focus on loved ones, expressed with deepest feelings and appreciation. By the time the basket returns to where it started, people are usually crying. It happens every year. It's a time of affirmation when we share our need for one another, and thank God for the family He has given us. This experience becomes more meaningful each year because of the inexorable march of time and its effect on the older generations among us. We have been painfully aware in recent years that some special people are now absent from the family circle, Jim's parents and my uncle. But we are grateful for each member of our small family who has survived another year.

I am reminded at this moment of a prayer expressed by Jim's father during the final year of his life. We had been to Kansas City for a visit and were on the way to the airport at the end of that pleasant vacation. Jim asked his dad to say a prayer before we were separated. I'll never forget his words, spoken in the car as we approached the airport.

He said, "Lord, we have enjoyed being together so much this past week, and you have been good to make this time possible. But Lord, we are realistic enough to know that life moves on, and that circumstances will not always be as we enjoy them today. We understand that a day is coming when the fellowship we now share will be but a memory to those who remain. That's why I want to thank you for bringing love into our lives for this season, and for the happiness we have experienced with one another."

Two weeks later, my father-in-law suffered a massive heart attack from which he never recovered. And his final prayer is his legacy to us today. Circumstances will inevitably change; nothing in this life is eternal or permanent. But while God grants us breath, we will enjoy one another to the fullest and spread our love as far and wide as possible.

Thanksgiving at the Dobson home is an occasion for the celebration of that philosophy.

THANKSGIVING HOSPITALITY

- As a loving tradition, invite a few guests to dinner who have no family and nowhere to go on Thanksgiving Day.

- A few days before Thanksgiving, ask each guest to recall two or three of his or her favorite dishes.

- Serve one of each guest's favorite dishes with your turkey dinner. Your guests will be *delightfully* thankful for your hospitality.

CREATE A "CENTERPIECE"

As a family project, create your own traditional centerpiece to be used each year on your Thanksgiving table. It can be as simple or as complex as you choose. Be creative! The family will enjoy seeing the arrangement year after year.

SUGGESTIONS

Pilgrim salt and pepper shakers
Papier-mâché turkey
Paper-folded turkey
Horn of plenty filled with fresh fruits,
    vegetables, and nuts
Dried flower arrangement

"THANK YOU" PLACE CARDS

- Fold unlined 3" x 5" cards in half to make place cards for every person at the Thanksgiving table.

- Decorate the cards in a Thanksgiving theme.

- Write each person's name on the front of a card.

- On the inside, write a personal thank-you message. Make each message personal, truthful, and specific, for example: "You always remember my birthday," "Thank you for being such a thoughtful aunt," etc.

NOTE: Larger cards can be used if desired so that each member of the family can write a message to every other person having dinner—all on the same card. Each individual then receives more than one expression of gratitude and from more than one person. It's fun to know just what makes others appreciate you.

"I'M THANKFUL FOR . . ."

- Play the game "Twenty Questions," basing it on things for which each person is thankful, such as a favorite food, home, pet, country, etc.

- The person who is "it" thinks of one thing for which he or she is thankful, and the others try to guess what it is by asking questions he or she can answer yes or no.

- If the group cannot guess the answer in twenty questions or less, the person who is "it" is the winner.

SPECIAL DAYS / THANKSGIVING

THANKS FOR WILDLIFE TREE

On Thanksgiving, after dinner is finished, christen the Christmas season by decorating the first tree—an outdoor Christmas gift for the wildlife in your neighborhood. Make any or all of the following suggestions and use them to trim the tree. There will be many hours of delightful bird-and squirrel-watching as you share these gifts with God's creatures.

SUGGESTED MATERIALS

    ground suet
    stale bread crumbs
    bird seed
    emptied orange or grapefruit halves
    pipe cleaners
    pine cones
    peanut butter
    cranberries
    popped corn
    raisins
    15" pieces of floral wire
    peanuts (unshelled and unsalted)
    heavy thread
    stale doughnuts

- Protect your working area with newspaper or plastic before assembling the gifts described below.

- Mix ground suet with seeds or stale bread crumbs and fill empty orange or grapefruit halves with the mixture. Attach pipe cleaners at three places around the edge; join them at the center and twist to form a hook to hang the feeder on branches.

- Spread pine cones with peanut butter and roll them in bird seed. Attach a pipe cleaner for a hanger.

- String cranberries, popcorn, and raisins on pieces of floral wire. Bend wire and attach ends to form a circle that can be hung over the ends of the branches.

- Tie peanuts along a piece of heavy thread and tie onto tree.

- Tie stale doughnuts to tree with thread or floral wire.

MELTED CRAYON ART

- From the old crayons that may have accumulated among your children's toys, gather up a selection in fall colors.

- Use a crayon sharpener or vegetable peeler to turn the crayons into shavings. Keep colors separate in small paper cups or baby-food jars.

- On art paper or manila paper, draw an outline of a Thanksgiving object such as a turkey, pumpkin, horn of plenty, fall leaf, etc.

- Place the drawing on an ironing board, first protecting the ironing board cover with a layer of waxed paper. Lightly sprinkle shavings to color in areas of picture.

- Carefully cover the picture with waxed paper.

- Iron carefully, using an iron on low heat, and apply pressure just long enough to melt the shavings onto the paper.

- Allow the drawing to cool slightly.

- Remove the waxed paper and hang your work of art. You may want to cut out your drawing before hanging.

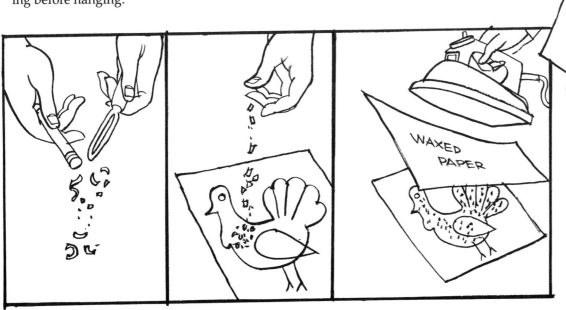

SPECIAL DAYS / THANKSGIVING

MEMORIES OF A SPECIAL CHRISTMAS

If everything special and warm and happy in my formative years could have been consolidated into one word, that word would have been *Christmas*. So, by the time the building blocks of my days had piled themselves into something as formidable as late adolescence, Christmas had a lot to live up to.

Christmas, by then, meant fireplaces and the bustle of a big excited family, complete with aunts, uncles, and cousins. It meant great smells from the kitchen—homemade bread and cranberries bubbling on the stove, pumpkin pies and turkey. It meant Grandma's cheery voice racing to be the first to holler "Christmas Gift!" as we came in the door. It meant real cedar Christmas trees, handmade foil ornaments, and lots of secrets. It meant enfolding in the arms of our great family the lonely or forsaken of our village who had no place to go. It meant all the good and lovely things we said about Christmas being in the heart and the joy being in the giving.

Then came that other year.

There were many things that conspired, as it were, to bring me to the laboratory situation in which I would test all my so glibly accepted theories. Grandma was gone, leaving in my heart a vacuum that wouldn't go away. My sister was married now and had the responsibility of sharing her holidays with her husband's people. The other relatives were far away. After a lifetime of serving in the ministry, Daddy had that year felt directed to resign his flock with no other pastures in mind and "wait on the Lord." Since I was away at college, just beginning my first year, I wasn't there when my parents moved from the parsonage to the tiny cottage at the lake which a concerned businessman had helped them build. Nor was I prepared that winter day for the deserted barrenness that can be found in resort areas built only for summertime fun.

There was no fireplace. There was no bustle of a big excited family. Gone was the sense of tradition and history that is the art of the aged to provide, and gone was the thrill of the immediate future that comes with the breathless anticipation of children.

The dinner was going to be small, for just the three of us, and there wasn't any ring in the brave attempt at shouting "Christmas Gift!" that Mother made as I came in the door. Daddy suggested that because I'd always

loved it, he and I should go to the woods to cut our own tree. I knew that now, of all times, I could not let my disappointment show. I put on my boots and my cheeriest face, and off through the knee-deep snow we trudged into the Michigan woods. My heart was heavy, and I knew Mother was back at the stove fighting back the tears for all that was not there.

There was loveliness as the forest lay blanketed in its heavy comforter of snow, but there was no comforter to wrap around the chill in my heart. Daddy whistled as he chopped the small cedar tree. (He always whistled when there was something bothering him.) As the simple tuneless melody cut through the silent frozen air, I got a hint of the silent burdens adults carry, and for the first time felt myself on the brink of becoming one. So as I picked up my end of the scraggly, disappointingly small cedar, I also picked up my end of grownup responsibility. I felt the times shift. I was no longer a child to be sheltered and cared for and entertained. My folks had put good stuff in me. Now as I trudged back through the snow, watching the back of my father's head, the weary curve of his shoulders, his breath making smoke signals in the morning air, I vowed to put some good stuff back into their lives.

The day was somehow different after that. We sat around our little tree stringing cranberries and making foil cut-outs. But this time it was not the activity of a child, but sort of a ceremonial tribute to the child I somehow could never again afford to be, and to the people who had filled that childhood with such wealth and beauty.

CHRISTMAS TRADITIONS TO TRY

- Start a tree-decorating tradition. Serve the same menu each year as you trim the tree. The children will look forward to it. (Menu suggestions: clam chowder and bread sticks; Christmas cookies and hot chocolate; Christmas cake and hot cider.)

- Each Christmas, let each of your children choose or make his or her own tree ornament. When they are grown, their ornaments will have special memories as they trim their own "family tree."

- Each Christmas, start a tradition of viewing all the family photographs, slides, and movies. It's fun to see how everyone has changed, and it stirs warm memories to reminisce about when the pictures were taken.

- On December 1, set up a card table with an appropriate jigsaw puzzle (500–1,000 pieces). As guests drop in throughout the holidays, they will enjoy working on the project. The object is to complete the puzzle by Christmas.

- Set a date with another family to go caroling in the neighborhood. Close the evening with refreshments.

- Parents give elementary age children $20 each to buy Christmas presents for *everyone*. (You may need to adjust for inflation.) Help children start a Christmas savings fund for next year, putting aside something each month from their allowance.

- Honor Jesus with a special birthday party (see next page).

SPECIAL DAYS / CHRISTMAS

JESUS' BIRTHDAY PARTY

Have a party in honor of Him whose birth we celebrate. Include in the celebration an older person who would otherwise be alone, someone you have just met, a young person away from home, and one or two very special friends such as a pastor or teacher who is important to your family's life.

Some special things to make or do might include:

- Birthday-card place cards.

- A special star-shaped cake with white and yellow icing full of fruit to represent the fulfillment of the seed of promise.

- A table centerpiece of a basket or small wooden box of clean straw surrounded by small packages made to represent gold, frankincense, and myrrh. Someone might tell about the three gifts and what they might have represented or how they might have been used.

EXAMPLE: Gold was the most precious metal, symbol of God's most precious gift. Perhaps this provided the financial means for the trip Mary, Joseph, and Jesus made to Egypt and for their stay there when they were forced to hide from Herod.

Frankincense and myrrh were important spices used in Jewish rituals as incense and as burial spices. Perhaps these gifts hinted at the fulfillment of the old Law as well as the crucifixion of Jesus that was to come. Someone has suggested that Mary may have kept these precious spices and used them to embalm the body of our Lord thirty-three years after His birth.

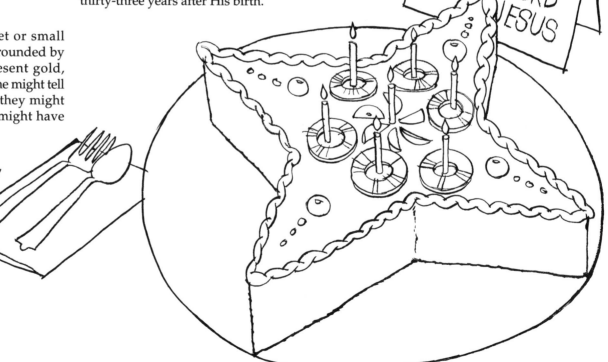

CHRISTMAS CARD ACTIVITIES

CHRISTMAS CARD DEVOTIONS

Cards can be used as a meaningful part of family devotions during the Advent season.

- Each day (or on selected days) use the cards received on that particular day, or have someone pull a specific number of cards from a basket used for this purpose.

- During family devotions, or after singing or Bible study, read the cards aloud.

- Have prayer for the families who sent the cards.

- Hang the cards up for display on the mantel, around a doorway or archway, on the back of a door, or on the Christmas tree.

CHRISTMAS CARD PRAYER LINK

Use Christmas cards as a link to real people and their needs through the Christmas season and the month of January.

- Choose one Christmas card each day from those received. Read the whole card aloud and pass it around the family circle. (Do this at a regular time like bedtime or after supper each night or at breakfast time.)

- Have special prayer together for each person in the family that sent the card.

- Send a postcard to that family to tell them about your Christmas-card prayers and that their card was the one chosen on this day. They will appreciate knowing that your family prayed for their family.

AFTER-CHRISTMAS CARDS

- As Christmas cards come, place them in an attractive container. After Christmas is over and the household is more settled, place the container near the dinner table.

- After dinner, pass the container and let each member of the family choose one card.

- Take turns reading the cards and enjoying their beauty.

- Discuss the family or person who sent the card. Are there any specific problems or needs?

- Close your dinner hour by praying for the families or persons who sent the cards.

SPECIAL DAYS / CHRISTMAS

HOMEMADE CHRISTMAS DECORATIONS

GARLANDS FOR THE HOUSE

Make these garlands on evenings before Christmas to use on your Christmas tree or in your hallway, doorways, or stairway:

- Lifesaver garland

  1. Cut two equal strands of desired length of colorful yarn.
  2. String Lifesaver candies loosely on the first strand.
  3. Lay the string of candy on a table, making the Lifesavers lie flat, in one direction, end to end.
  4. With the other strand of yarn weave in and out in the opposite direction so that each candy is forced to lie flat.
  5. Secure ends of each yarn to last candy on each end.

- String Cheerios or other circular cereal pieces in the same way, using brightly colored yarn or ribbon. Be prepared to replace the garlands as they are nibbled away.

- String raw cranberries and popcorn alternately onto a piece of yarn. Use a darning needle to pull the yarn through the berry or kernel (younger children will need adult supervision).

- String colored marshmallows randomly or in a predetermined pattern of colors.

- Make a garland of white foam packing squiggles. Watch that children do not put these in their mouths; this foam is *not* edible.

- String uncooked elbow macaroni and other pasta, painting it if desired.

HINT: Dip the end of the string or yarn in melted paraffin to make a "needle" that will be stiff and yet will bend as needed.

TREE AND PACKAGE ORNAMENTS

Take a special evening to create these ornaments to use as tree or package decorations.

- Cut shapes from cardboard and cover with foil or glitter.

- Hang sour gumdrop-type fruit slices with ornament hooks that have been inserted in the top of the candy.

- Hang white-chocolate-covered pretzels.

- Wrap popcorn balls in foil or colored cellophane. Secure the wrapping with bright yarn, leaving the ends long enough for tying the balls onto the tree.

- Make cornstarch-and-soda clay ornaments from recipe on page 85.

  1. While dough is warm, divide it into two portions. Use food coloring to color one red, the other green.
  2. Roll dough on waxed paper and cut into Christmas shapes with cookie cutters.
  3. Poke a large nail through the top of each ornament to make a hole for hanging.
  4. Dry thoroughly, turning ornaments occasionally.
  5. If desired, glue glitter to parts of ornaments.

DECK THE HALLS

- Cover a large foam ball with sprigs of mistletoe and hang it in an archway or doorway as an excuse for family hugs and kisses. As the mistletoe dries, take care to pick up any berries that may fall, as these are poisonous and may be ingested by small children. Some floral stores now sell silk or plastic mistletoe. This might be a safer choice if you have little ones.

- Have the family make a special time of arranging the nativity set.

- Tie ripple ribbon on the ends of cellophane-wrapped mints, then tie them onto a foam wreath.

- Make homemade taffy (see recipe, page 114). Wrap in waxed paper bits and twist ends. Tie on the tree or a styrofoam wreath with yarn or string.

- Make large letters out of newspaper or construction paper spelling out "HAPPY BIRTHDAY, JESUS." Tape to a large front window. Or make a computer-generated banner and decorate it in holiday colors.

- Have each member of the family whittle from balsa wood a "Christ-mon" (Christ-monogram) such as a fish, cross, manger, star, lamb, etc. Talk about the meanings of the chosen symbols as you hang them on your tree.

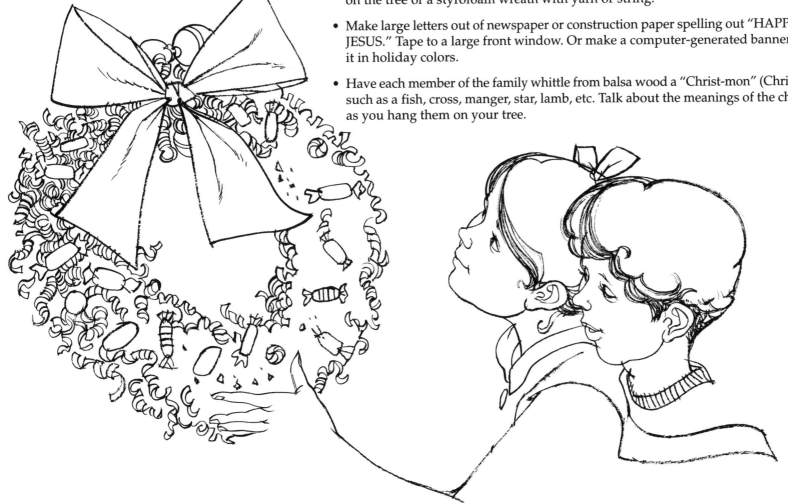

SPECIAL DAYS / CHRISTMAS

MAGAZINE CHRISTMAS ART

- From old magazines, tear pictures or ads that are mostly green.

- Cut the ads or pictures into pairs of strips of varying measured lengths, for example, 8 inches, 7 inches, 6 inches, 5 inches, etc.

- Turn a rectangular piece of poster board or construction paper so that the shorter sides are the top and bottom. Draw a vertical line from top to bottom midway between the left and right sides. Starting at the bottom with the longest strips of paper, glue one end of strips of equal length to each side of the vertical line (see diagram). As you add successive layers of shorter and shorter strips, slightly overlap the strips to avoid having the poster board or construction paper show through.

NOTE: This idea can be adapted to make a special Christmas card.

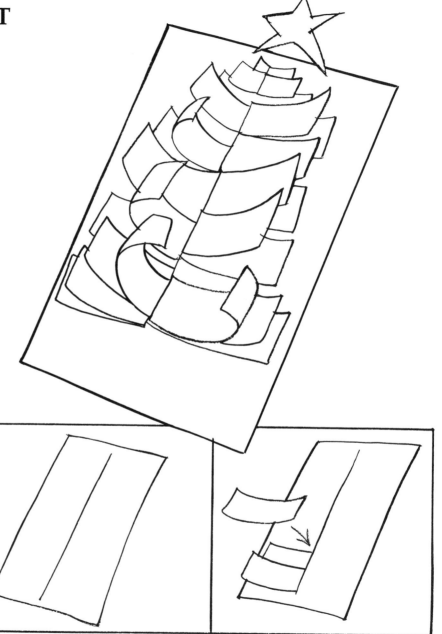

GROWING COLLECTION

As a part of the Christmas celebration every year, give each child an ornament of his or her own. When the children grow up and move into their own homes, they will have their own ornaments to take with them. These ornaments might be different for each child each year:

- crystal

- straw

- wood

- metal

- fancy designer ornament

- handmade

This collection is more than Christmas ornaments. Rather it is a collection of special memories, touched and treasured through the years.

SPECIAL DAYS / CHRISTMAS

CHRISTMAS . . . DOBSON STYLE

The Christmas season is greeted in the Dobson home with the same excitement that the approach of Thanksgiving brings. This wonderful occasion begins with decorating the house during the first week in December. Even though our children, Danae and Ryan, no longer live at home, they still come home to find their large red and green Christmas stockings hanging on either side of the fireplace. Early each Christmas morning, these are filled with inexpensive small gifts, nuts, candies, and fruits. We still set aside a few days before Christmas for baking our traditional cookies and candies, not only for the family but for neighbors and friends. This emphasizes to our children the spirit of giving. As Ryan used to say, "I love Christmas because everyone in the neighborhood is always sharing."

Then comes the special night when we go as a family to pick out the Christmas tree. I look for a fir with the best shape, and Jim looks for the best price! Having made the selection, we designate an evening to add the decorations. Excitement fills the room as the lights are strung on the tree and we begin hanging red balls and dozens of specially selected ornaments that I have collected over the years. The house resounds with traditional Christmas music, and we drink hot chocolate and munch our home-baked Christmas cookies and candies. (Is it any wonder that Christmas is such a fattening time in the Dobson household?)

When our children were younger they each had their own "tree"—a small artificial fir which they decorated with lights and their own ornaments. They have become much too sophisticated to continue the tradition, but their memories of the occasion are still warm and meaningful.

Much about the holidays has changed as our children have grown. But much has stayed the same. Since we live in Colorado now and our extended family, for the most part, is in California, some of our traditions have been modified. We still eat Chinese food some years on Christmas Eve. (Don't ask me how that tradition started, or more important, why?) Later, Ryan, Danae, and their grandparents gather around the fireplace with Jim and me, and Jim reads from the Bible. After discussing the passage, we do something very meaningful. The lights are lowered and I give each family member a votive candle. I explain as we take our turns igniting our candles that the light represents Jesus who was born into a dark world to give us eternal life. As we light our candles, we share one blessing during the past year we are especially thankful for and something we are asking God to do in our lives during the upcoming new year—perhaps a spiritual goal for the year. We then blow out our candles and Jim closes our time together with a prayer. Then we all get to select and open one gift from under the tree.

On Christmas morning, we have our traditional Christmas brunch, consisting of warm cinnamon rolls, orange juice, and coffee. When the big moment arrives, we sit around the tree, opening our presents one at a time in an effort to preserve this happy moment as long as possible.

Finally, we gather at the dining table for our Christmas dinner of turkey, dressing, cranberry sauce, mashed potatoes, two kinds of salads, and hot baked rolls. When we think we can't hold another bite, our traditional dessert of pound cake and ambrosia (a fruit dish with peeled grapes in it) is brought out. The family peels the grapes the evening before the meal. There's always laughter and warm family interaction during this activity. (The recipe for our ambrosia is provided on the opposite page, as well as the recipe for our traditional Christmas brunch cinnamon rolls.)

These happy days of Christmas come and go so quickly that we have sought a way to hold on to the pleasure a while longer. Therefore, we have developed a custom of saving our Christmas cards from friends and loved ones far and wide, and after New Year's Day, I put them on a tray near the dinner table. Every night we select some cards and read them, along with the letters enclosed with them. We then pray for those families around our table. This tradition may take months to complete, depending on the number of cards we receive. With the busy days of Christmas behind us, we can better enjoy the beauty of the cards and absorb the meaningful verses and personal notes.

The Christmas traditions that we have developed through the years are not unique to the Dobson household. Perhaps yours are similar in many respects. But they are extremely meaningful to each member of our family. These activities serve to emphasize the two vitally important themes that embody the Christmas spirit: celebration of Jesus' birth and life, and celebration of love for one another and for the entire human family. As such, this exciting time of the year brings out the very best that is within us.

CHRISTMAS MORNING BRUNCH
CINNAMON ROLLS (Serves 6)

    1 pkg. Pillsbury Crescent Dinner
       Rolls
       butter or margarine
       granulated sugar
       cinnamon
    1 small pkg. crushed pecans

Unroll dough into 4 rectangles (*do not* tear apart as in making crescent dinner rolls). Butter each rectangle generously. Then sprinkle on lots of sugar. Shake cinnamon on top. Add pecans. Roll into small logs and put in refrigerator for 3 minutes. Take out and slice into 1/4-inch thick pinwheels. Place on ungreased baking sheet, tucking pinwheel end under roll to prevent its unraveling while baking. Bake according to package instructions. Remove from oven and glaze. Make any powdered sugar glaze to spoon on top while rolls are still warm. Absolutely scrumptious with hot coffee or chocolate, crisp bacon, and scrambled eggs. Merry eating!

AMBROSIA (Serves 8)

    1 large bunch of green grapes
  4–6 large oranges
    1 large can crushed pineapple
    1 cup chopped pecans
  3–4 bananas
    1 cup granulated sugar
      whipping cream

Cut each grape in half. Take out seeds and peel off skin. (The men can do this around the table while the women are preparing the meal.) Cut peeling off oranges. Section orange slices and remove all white membrane. Cut each section of orange "meat" in half. Each chunk of orange should be about 1/4 inch. Add pineapple, pecans, sliced bananas, and sugar. Mix well. This should be really juicy. Serve in glass dessert dishes with sweetened whipping cream on top. We serve Christmas Ambrosia with pound cake—delicious! For another variation of this recipe see page 199.

CHRISTMAS GIFT IDEAS

- A rustic basket or wooden box (cheese or fruit box) lined with a colorful old-fashioned print fabric and filled with spools of thread in basic colors, bias tape, straight pins, needles, a thimble, seam ripper, tape measure, buttons in basic sizes.

- A handmade glasses case (leather, felt, needlepoint), filled with cleaning solution or tissues for glasses and a glasses repair kit.

- A bundle of extra long cinnamon sticks tied with a red and green plaid ribbon and a sprig of holly.

- A carpenter's extra long tape measure, a level, and a square (be sure metric measurements are included).

- A basket filled with shoe polish in basic colors, silicone protecting spray, shoeshine brush and cloth, and shoestrings.

- A stocking full of stockings: knee-socks for girls, athletic socks for boys, panty-hose for women, dress socks for men. Tie the stocking shut with a bright ribbon.

- A small tin tub lined with straw. Inside the tub pack a glass of homemade jelly and a matching glass containing a homemade spicy candle. A square of gingham tied with ribbon over the top of each jar will add color and personality.

- Several large bars of Ivory soap, a small craft knife, and a booklet on soap carving.

- A whole set of toothbrushes and toothpastes—one for each member of the family. (Be sure each person gets a different color brush.) These may be packed in a small shoebox wrapped in solid-color paper. Cut a big smile from red and white paper to put on the top of the box, or paint a smile directly on the box.

- A set of metric wrenches.

GIFTS OF TIME

• Each person gives a "gift of time" to every other member of the family. For example: a boy could offer to vacuum the carpet for his mom on the day of her choice, or a father could promise to take his son fishing at some future time.

• Write these time pledges on 3" x 5" cards and place them in envelopes for each person. The envelopes can then be hung on the Christmas tree and opened with the other gifts.

A PRESENT OF PRAISE

• Place a bookmark in the Bible where the Christmas story begins—Luke 2:1–20.

• Give each member of the family a pencil and sheet of paper. (Small children may color a picture.)

• Write (or color) a letter of praise and thanksgiving to Jesus, sharing from the heart. Place the letters with the Bible in a box and wrap as a Christmas present to be opened and shared on Christmas Eve.

CHRISTMAS "WISH BOOK"

• Give your child a mail-order catalog and two crayons of different colors.

• Let the child look through the pages for gifts he or she "wishes" to find under the Christmas tree. Use one color to mark first choice and another for second choice with gifts of similar type.

KEEPING THE SECRET

To keep the contents of a package secret, place the wrapped and properly tagged package inside a larger box. Pad with newspaper or tissue so there will be no rattling. Wrap outer package and label with another person's name. Do this with as many packages as you wish. When packages are unwrapped, the inner gift is given to the right person to open. Everyone will enjoy both surprises! (If you do not want to have to wrap two packages, try making a "quiet" package noisy by adding a few buttons or dried beans, or a light package heavy by adding a rock or other heavy object.)

SPECIAL DAYS / CHRISTMAS

MAKING CHRISTMAS EVE MEMORIES

Adapt any or all of the following to make a tradition of Christmas Eve for your family:

- Take a drive through town or a nearby large city to see the outdoor light displays.

- Read the Christmas story aloud from the Bible.

- Sing carols around the piano or sing with a favorite Christmas record.

- Have every family member take his or her turn giving some kind of Christmas performance.

- Attend a candlelight or watch night service. Make attending this special service an annual family affair.

- Let the children open one gift on Christmas Eve. (Perhaps this gift could be sleepwear to keep the children snuggly and warm on Christmas Eve.)

- Hang stockings (to be filled after children are asleep with such things as small toys, toothbrush, comb or brush, old-fashioned toys such as kaleidoscope, wooden top, jacks, pickup sticks, wooden flute, whistle, etc.). If you have small children, avoid toys with small parts that might cause choking.

- Serve hot wassail. A suggested recipe follows.

HOT WASSAIL

- In the base of a twelve-cup percolator put:

  **1 part cranapple juice
  5 parts apple cider (unpasteurized)**

- In the percolator basket put:

  **6–8 whole cloves
  2 cinnamon sticks
  2 tbsp. honey
  ¼ chopped lemon, including rind**

- Brew wassail as you normally would coffee.

- Or you may put the spices in the liquid and simmer in a crock-pot or a stovetop pan. To serve, dip the wassail with a ladle.

- Serve hot with a sliver of lemon or a cinnamon stick.

NOTE: If the family condones belief in Santa, the children could make a snack to leave out for him. Another nice tradition might be for Mom and Dad to have a glass of eggnog together after the children are in bed and take time to talk about love, blessings, goals, etc., or just enjoy a few quiet moments with each other.

MAKING CHRISTMAS MORNING EXTRA SPECIAL

- Take pictures of or videotape the children getting up on Christmas morning.

- Have the children stay in bed until Dad gives a special signal. (He could put a record on the stereo such as "Here Comes Santa Claus" or some other Christmas music.)

- Race to be the first to yell out some special phrase: "Christmas gift!" or "Merry Christmas!"

- Have a short worship time before opening gifts. Children could do this with parents being the "congregation."

- Have a special Christmas breakfast every year. A sample menu might include: fried apples, bagels, and cheese; blueberry muffins, scrambled eggs and bacon; or dried beef gravy on homemade biscuits. (Some families serve "chocolate gravy" that is similar to chocolate pudding, but thinner.)

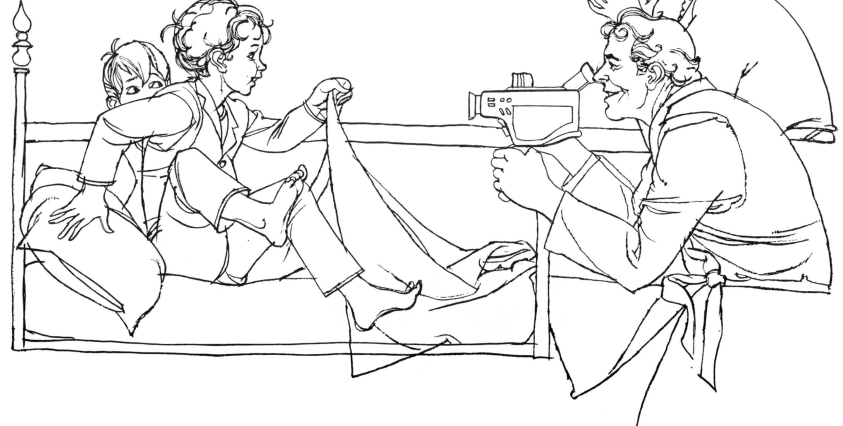

CHRISTMAS DAY REUNION

- Gather the family together for a reunion at the grandparents' home. Make it a "bring-in" dinner, everyone supplying his or her special dish so that no one has all the work!

- Choose one person to be "Santa" and pass out gifts. This might be the same person each time, or the honor could go to the youngest child or the youngest teenager; or all could "draw straws" for the honor.

- Celebrate by singing around the piano.

- Listen together as Grandfather or another older family member reads the Christmas story, or recite it together from Luke, chapter 2.

- Make plaster-of-Paris handprints each Christmas season. Paint with bright colors, shellac, or spray with fixative. Put name, year, and age on back. Save from year to year. See instructions on page 133 for making prints with plaster of Paris.

- Before Christmas dinner, put two fresh cranberries on each plate. After the family is seated, pass around a basket and, as cranberries are dropped in, share two ways in which Christmas is special to you. Follow by reading John 3:16, and conclude with prayer.

BIRTHDAY FLAG

Design and create a birthday flag for each person in the family—parents, too!

NOTE: This flag should be made of cloth so that it will last and should represent the person's favorite colors, interests, special abilities, hobbies, etc.

- Fly the flag from sunup to sundown on each person's birthday.

- Make a flag-raising and lowering ceremony by singing a favorite song, making up a cheer about him or her, etc.

- If a grandparent lives with the family or nearby, include him or her too.

SPECIAL DAYS / BIRTHDAYS

RYAN—SUNSHINE OF MY LIFE

"What are little boys made of? Frogs and snails and puppy dog tails . . . that's what little boys are made of."

Twenty-four years ago, a little boy named Ryan blessed our home with his presence. He has been a delight and a joy to our family since that moment. His personality radiates happiness in every room of our house, and his energy is boundless. As the evening nears and I begin to wear down, Ryan accelerates his pace and attacks the many activities that captivate his alert mind. Once in a while, I can corner him long enough to give him a hug.

Some years ago during the week of my birthday, our family decided to go for a leisurely stroll through our local shopping center. Ryan was only eight at the time, and he loved to visit the mall. He opened his piggybank and took out five dollars he had been saving for something special. As we walked along window shopping and enjoying being together, Ryan announced that he wanted to have some time alone to go to the toy store and pet shop. We set a time and place where we would meet and off he went. In about thirty minutes, he came walking up with a grin that stretched from ear to ear.

Ryan said, "Here, Mom, this is for your birthday—you can open it right, now."

I answered, "But, Ryan, it isn't my birthday yet. Can I save it and open it on Friday?"

By the look on his face it was obvious that he felt very strongly about my opening the gift right there in the center of the shopping mall. He announced it cost *a lot* of money (he had spent the entire five dollars on it). I carefully opened the package and was filled with emotion as I gazed with tenderness on its contents. The gift was not one that you would expect to receive from an eight-year-old boy. He had bought me a lovely desk set. The ostrich-feathered white pen looked like an old-fashioned quill that Ben Franklin might have used to sign the Declaration of Independence. The stand was padded in matching white, with a spray of pink flowers delicately painted around the edges. I was so touched that my eyes brimmed with tears as I hugged and thanked my son for such an extravagant gift. It has been many years since that day and I still treasure that pen as a reminder of Ryan's spontaneous gift of love.

There are times in our lives when the cost of parenting seems staggeringly high! No matter how you look at it, children are emotionally exhausting, time-consuming, sometimes frustrating, and always maddeningly complex. In fact, their developmental years are governed entirely by "Murphy's Law." For example, if they drop a slice of bread on the carpet, it will inevitably land buttered-side down. And when they catch the flu, they never vomit in the bathroom. They turn up their noses at their oatmeal and gag at the sight of their eggs, but enthusiastically drink the dog's water and float their rubber duckies in the toilet, etc. I'm sure you could add to this list of childhood "Murphyisms."

But in moments when you are touched by the soul of a child, as I was through Ryan's act of love, you suddenly realize the eternal significance of these precious years. Then, no other task on earth seems quite as important or meaningful as raising and training and guiding him through his developmental experiences.

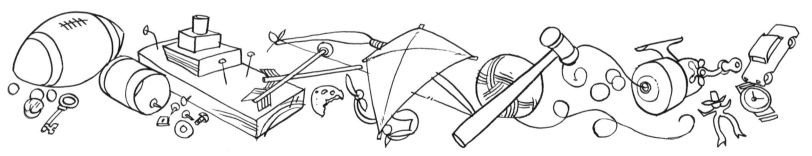

SPECIAL FROM BEGINNING TO END

- Choose one gift and put it at the birthday person's place at the breakfast table to be opened as soon as his or her day begins.

- Ask the birthday person to plan the menu for supper. Give it to the family at this time so that his or her wishes can be carried out. (Or, let the birthday person choose a favorite eating place, as the budget allows.)

- Make sure the birthday person has fresh clean sheets to sleep on for the birthday night.

ANNUAL BIRTHDAY INTERVIEW

- On each child's birthday, record on cassette or videotape an interview with him or her. Ask him or her to describe special memories about the past year—happy times, sad moments, fun things that happened, and other meaningful experiences.

- Add to the recording every year at the time of each birthday.

- After each interview, play back the previous years' conversations.

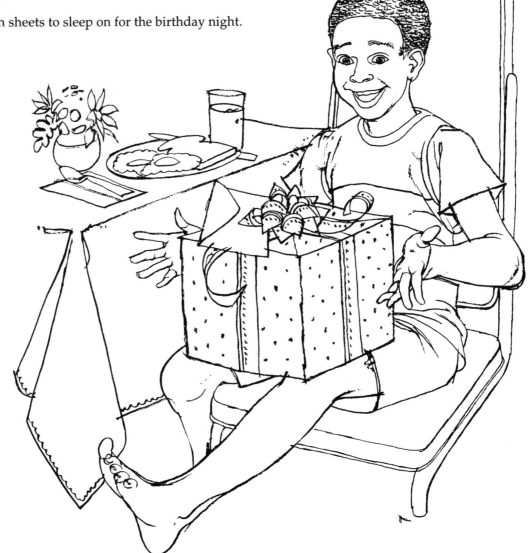

CREATIVE GIFTS

Here are some ideas for very special birthday gifts:

- Tickets to the zoo, a concert, a craft show, a film.

- A prepaid motel reservation for parents of young children (so they can rediscover each other alone) and you volunteer to babysit!

- A pretty basket containing gardening gloves, small shovel, flower seeds, liquid fertilizer, etc.

- A large roll of adhesive tape for a young child (aged four to seven) who seldom is allowed to have tape to use as he or she wishes.

- A poem written especially for the "birthday person," perhaps mounted on a pretty piece of wood or written by hand in ink in the front of an "empty book" for writing about special moments all year long. (Available at stationery stores.)

- A cassette tape containing a song or message about the birthday person.

- A set of handmade gingham napkins, colorfully displayed in a bread or cracker basket.

- A basket of fragrant soaps, tied with a ribbon to match the bathroom. (This gift is equally welcomed by men, women, and children. Choose masculine or juvenile soaps and ribbon for men or children.)

- A cassette made by the birthday person's baby, child, or parents or children who are far away from home.

- A beach towel.

- A swim mask, nose plugs, swim fins.

- A crockware jug, tin bucket, or wooden pail filled with dried flowers, colorful wash cloths, dish towels, cattails, spices.

- A kerosene lamp with lamp oil, a hand-crocheted table scarf, and an old book from a flea market.

- Two or three colorful belts.

- A stapler and two or three boxes of staples (for kids, too, if they're used with supervision!).

- Art supplies.

A KID'S FAVORITE

RED RASPBERRY BIRTHDAY CAKE

1 pkg. white cake mix
2 tbsp. flour
1 red raspberry Jell-O, regular size

•

$^1/_2$ cup water
1 cup vegetable oil
4 eggs
1 10-oz. pkg. frozen red
    raspberries, divided

•

1 box confectioner's sugar
1 stick margarine or butter

Mix together the dry cake mix, flour, and raspberry Jell-O. Combine the water and vegetable oil and add to the dry mixture. Add the four eggs one at a time, mixing well. Stir in *half* the frozen red raspberries.

HINT: Cut block of raspberries in half while still frozen so that exactly half can be saved for icing.

Pour batter into three greased and floured 8-inch round layer-cake pans. Bake at 325 degrees for 20 minutes or until cake feels bouncy in the center.

For icing, combine the softened butter or margarine, confectioner's sugar, and reserved half of the raspberries, thawed. Mix together with electric mixer. Spread on cooled cake.

SPECIAL DAYS / BIRTHDAYS

SPECIAL DAYS / BIRTHDAYS

SPECIAL BIRTHDAY PARTIES

"DO-IT-YOURSELF" BIRTHDAY PARTY

- Plan a birthday party for six or eight children, ages ten and younger.

- Look in your cookbook for a yummy ginger-bread cookie recipe and assemble the ingredients needed to make it, along with the necessary utensils.

- When the guests arrive, let them help you make gingerbread boy cookies. Each child can then take home the cookie he or she made.

ADOPTED BIRTHDATE

- Celebrate an "extra" birthday on the date your adopted son/daughter came to be your child. The attention he receives on that day is designed to make him know his adoption was a blessed event to be celebrated rather than a dark secret to be hidden. This second birthday makes adopted children feel special.

INSTANT PARTY FOR A LOVED ONE AWAY FROM HOME

- Bake cookies and arrange them in a box with packets of fruit-punch mix, party napkins, and paper cups.

- Wrap the box in birthday paper with a card explaining that you are sending an "instant party."

- Finish with an outer wrapping of brown paper and mail to that special birthday person.

HAPPY "HALF" BIRTHDAY

- On each child's "half" birthday, have a half celebration: at age two and a half, three and a half, etc.

- Bake a "half" cake and serve a half glass of punch. Give the child money for half a toy and let him earn the other half. He will be delightfully surprised.

THE GIFT OF WHAT YOU ARE

- Collect small gift boxes (the size jewelry comes in) or small matchboxes.

- On narrow strips of bright paper about four inches long, have each member of the family write "I love you because . . ." and sign his or her name on the back. Each person may contribute as many as he wishes.

- Roll strips tightly and seal the end with a tiny dot of rubber cement. Wrap the scroll with a twist-tie (from a box of plastic storage bags) until it dries.

- Put scrolls on end in the small box, then wrap or decorate the box.

- Give the gift to the birthday person to read now or to save for special "low" days. Great medicine to counteract discouragement all year long!

NOTE: This gift is very special for someone away at college or in the service.

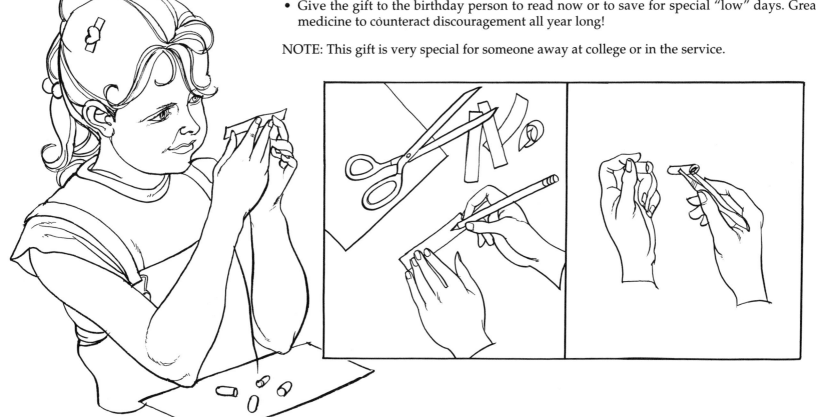

BAKED POTATO SUPPER

- Wrap large potatoes in aluminum foil and bake them in the oven about one hour at 350 degrees. Time the baking so the potatoes are just done when everyone arrives.

- Prepare all kinds of trappings and set them out buffet style so that everyone can fix his or her own potato.

  two or three kinds of grated cheese
  chives
  crumbled bacon
  chopped green peppers
  chopped onion
  cooked and drained hamburger bits
  cooked and drained sausage bits
  sliced ripe olives
  sour cream
  butter
  chopped peanuts
  sunflower seeds

- Serve cold drinks and coffee or iced tea.

GOD'S DAY IS SPECIAL

- Celebrate the Day of Worship with a special tablecloth or placemats used at breakfast or lunch *only* on that day.

- The mats can be sewn by Mom, or the children can make their own from construction paper and colorfully decorate them with crayons or marker pens.

- This tradition will help the family recognize that the Day of Worship is special because it is God's Day.

SPECIAL DAY TOYS

- Choose or buy five or six toys or games that delight a child.

- Save these to be used or played with only on the Lord's Day.

- Since there is more time to enjoy each other on this day, make a special effort to play with your child and his or her special toys and games.

SPECIAL DAY MUSIC

- Use music to make the Day of Worship special by playing only Christian or classical music on this day.

- Sing a familiar chorus, hymn, or verse together as a grace for dinner on the Day of Worship.

- Read the history of a familiar hymn as part of the family worship. Then sing the hymn together.

- Make this a treat by also doing special things together as a family while music is playing, for example:

    – Make chocolate-chip cookies.
    – Play Scrabble, Boggle, or other word games.
    – Paint or sculpt.
    – Do a huge jigsaw puzzle.
    – Play the music together on the various instruments your family plays.

SPECIAL DAYS / DAY OF WORSHIP

SPECIAL SUPPER

If the main meal on the Day of Worship is at noon, have the suppertime or evening after-church snack be a prepared-by-Dad special. Try the following idea for a starter:

DAD'S CHEESE MELTS

- Start with slices of buttered crunchy wheat bread and mild Colby cheese.

- Melt cheese on bread in oven until cheese is bubbly.

- Serve on paper plates with chunks of dill pickle and glasses of cold milk.

SAND DOLLAR REMEMBRANCE

- When someone becomes a Christian and receives Jesus into his or her life, commemorate the occasion by giving the new Christian a sand dollar. (Read about the symbol of the sand dollar and the tiny "birds" inside, then share the story with the new Christian. Many gift stores and Christian bookstores sell cards and plaques describing the legend.)

- As a remembrance of this special occasion, date the object with a waterproof pen.

- Each year on the anniversary of the date, bring attention to that important decision with a special prayer before dinner.

- For another remembrance of this important event, take a photograph of the person on his or her day of decision. Document the relevant information on the back of the picture.

- Place your own sand dollar in a prominent place such as on a nightstand, kitchen counter, window sill, etc., to remind you of the day you became a Christian.

THE LEGEND OF THE SAND DOLLAR

The sand dollar is more than a beautiful marine animal; it also symbolizes three important events in the life of Christ. The small star in the center signifies the bright star that shone over Bethlehem on the night of Jesus' birth. The large pattern on the sand dollar's underside is known as the Christmas poinsettia.

The five holes in the sand dollar represent the five wounds inflicted upon Jesus during His crucifixion, and the petals of the Easter lily, extending outward from the star, symbolize His resurrection. Break the sand dollar apart and you will find five white "doves" reminding us of the dove that appeared after Jesus' baptism.

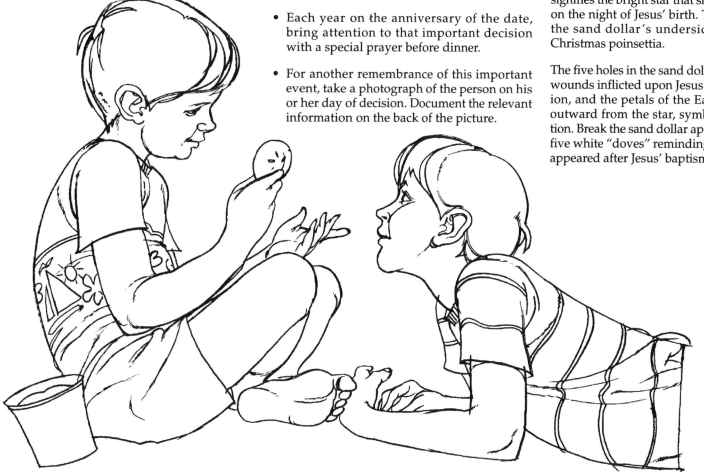

SPECIAL DAYS / DAY OF WORSHIP

BLACK SUNDAY

The following article appeared originally in my husband's book, *Straight Talk to Men and Their Wives,* and is adapted here with the permission of Word, Incorporated.

Is Sunday morning a particularly difficult time in your home? For some reason, the Sabbath can be the most frustrating day of the week for our family, especially during the "get 'em ready for church" routine. But Black Sunday was uniquely chaotic! We began that day by getting up too late, meaning everyone had to rush to get to church on time. That produced emotional pressure, especially for Jim and me. Then there was the matter of spilled milk at breakfast, and the black shoe polish on the floor. And, of course, Ryan got dressed first, enabling him to slip out the back door and get himself dirty from head to toe. It was necessary to take him down to the skin and start over with clean clothes once more. Instead of handling these irritants as they arose, we began criticizing one another and hurling accusations back and forth. At least one spanking was delivered, as I recall, and another three or four were promised. Yes, it was a day to be remembered (or forgotten). Finally, four harried people managed to stumble into church, ready for a great spiritual blessing, no doubt. There's not a pastor in the world who could have moved us on that morning.

I felt guilty throughout the day for the strident tone of our home on that Black Sunday. Sure, our children shared the blame, but they were merely responding to our disorganization. We had overslept, and that's where the conflict originated.

After the evening service, we called the family together around the kitchen table. We began by describing the kind of day we had had, and asked each person to forgive us for our part in it. Furthermore, we said that we thought we should give each member of the family an opportunity to say whatever he or she was feeling inside.

Ryan was given the first shot, and he fired it at me. "You've been a real grouch today, Mom!" he said with feeling. "You've blamed me for everything I've done all day long."

I then explained why I had been unhappy with him, trying not to be defensive about his charges.

Danae then poured out her hostilities and frustrations. Finally, Jim and I had an opportunity to explain the tensions that had caused our overreaction.

It was a valuable time of ventilation and honesty that drew us together once more. We then had prayer as a family and asked the Lord to help us live and work together in love and harmony.

Every family has moments when they violate all the rules—even departing from the Christian principles by which they have lived. Fatigue itself can damage all the high ideals that have been recommended to parents in seminars, books, and sermons. The important question is, how do mothers and fathers reestablish friendship within their families when the storm has passed? Open, non-threatening discussion offers one solution to that situation.

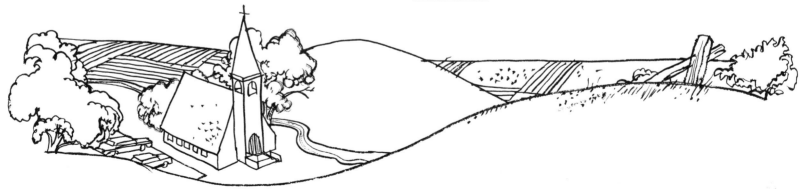

FAMILY NIGHT*

Designate one evening a week as family night. If you have a special activity such as roller skating that the whole family enjoys doing together, you might plan to do that on the night you have chosen.

Try to make family night the same day every week so that every family member will keep that night free when making individual plans.

If you don't have special plans for family night, bring out the fun box.

HOW TO MAKE A FUN BOX

- Get a box; a shoebox or empty round oatmeal box is the best.

- Decorate the outside together, labeling the box "Family Fun Box."

- Have each family member write down on slips of paper something to do as a family. These activities could include:

    bowling
    reading a book aloud
    seeing a movie
    sending out for pizza
    going for a bike ride

- When the designated evening rolls around, pull a slip of paper from the fun box and do whatever it tells you.

- Replenish the slips of paper either by replacing the slip just drawn or by adding to the box as family members come up with additional ideas.

*See list of Memory-Making Resources on page 220.

THE MAGIC HOUR

If you have children of school age, make it a rule for one parent to be home when the children arrive home from school.

This is the moment for maximum communication. . . .

HINTS

- Do baking at this hour or just before so that the house always smells wonderful—like someone's there who loves you!

- Play music that denotes joy and peace.

- Have nutritious snacks ready as a convenient option to junk foods—carrot and celery sticks, sunflower seeds and raisins, orange juice.

- Be prepared to listen enthusiastically.

- Give at least half-an-hour "wind-down" time before requiring practice of musical instruments, homework, or chores.

- Try to discourage television at this hour by having more interesting options.

TOGETHERNESS

HOMEWORK

- Work is always more fun when loved ones do it together. Sit down with your children during their homework hour and use this time to answer correspondence, work on the family album, or catch up on the mending. The children will concentrate better, and parents will be there to answer any questions that might arise.

- A time of play (a table game or a walk around the block) is an ideal follow-up to the time of shared discipline.

TEEN TALK

As a teenager's schedule becomes more hectic, it is important to make time for parent and child to keep talking together. Here are some ways to save time for each other:

- Save the last fifteen minutes before bedtime to share together in the teenager's room. A middle-of-the-bed picnic of popcorn or peanuts and a beverage can be a special treat as you talk about the day. ("Tucking in" time is not just for young children.) This is a good time to read a verse of Scripture or page from a devotional book together, with the teenager, not the parent, doing the choosing and reading.

- An out-of-town, one-day vacation or shopping spree is a good time to talk. At times this may warrant getting the teenager out of school for a special day, especially if it is a high-stress time. Sometimes kids need a

break, too. (The parent should not take another adult along to talk to, but should just delight in the company of this child who is becoming an adult and a new friend.)

- Save Sundays. Try not to overschedule the "Lord's Day," but keep it free for family time. Parents who honor this day can more easily expect growing children to save this time. Be ready to listen to good music, do art projects, take walks, etc.

- Biking and hiking provide good opportunities for communication, especially between one parent and one teenager at a time. Other times it's fun to have the whole family.

- Be spontaneous. A fish fry at midnight, a breakfast in the park, a surprise lunch date away from school, a surprise gift when it's nobody's birthday, a special privilege—all these can open the door for real communication.

- Take lessons together—horseback riding, archery, tennis, basket weaving, ceramics, skiing, cake decorating—or take up a new interest like drag racing, fishing, tennis, skeet shooting, mountain climbing, dress designing. Often the teenager will excel and have the new experience of helping a parent master the new skill.

- Keep on hugging and touching. It is a terrible shock to children to have the hugging stop just at the age when they need it most. Avoid saying, "You're too old for that." Let teenagers cry, giggle, sit on your lap, kiss you good-night, or talk into the wee hours of the morning.

CONVERSATIONAL TENNIS

- Supply yourself with half a dozen or more tennis balls.

- Ask your elementary school child to sit on a chair on the opposite side of the room from you.

- Throw him a tennis ball, but ask him to catch it and hold it in his lap. Then toss him another and another.

- Sit and look at one another for a few moments until he asks you to explain your point.

- Then say, "It isn't much of a game until you throw the balls back to me, is it?" Continue to show him how conversation is also a game that requires people to toss their ideas back and forth. Explain that if you merely "catch" the other person's comment, but don't return it with one of your own, that's like holding the tennis balls in your lap; it ruins the fun.

- Practice "tossing" words back and forth with your child. You may say, for example, "Did you have a good day in school?" If the child says, "Yeah," in return, he has merely caught your words. But if he says, "Yes, I got an A in math," he has learned to throw you a comment of his own.

- Discuss how well the child returns adult comments the next time he plays conversational tennis with friends and associates.

PLAY TOGETHER

Use your children as a wonderful excuse to play! Hardly ever is TV worth watching if, in order to do so, the family has to give up time that could be spent playing together. Try some of the following ideas or ideas of your own.

Inside:

flash cards
Fish
Old Maid
Boggle
Scrabble
Twister
Monopoly
Sorry
Clue
Pit
Flinch
Jenga

Outside:

walks
races
sledding
croquet
badminton
tennis
basketball
kickball*
volleyball
hopscotch
jump rope
roller skating

Kids talk when they play, and they don't have to get your attention if they already have it!

No game is important in itself. Playing together is what counts. Remember, poor sportsmanship doesn't always come from the kids.

* Played like softball, except that the pitcher rolls a volleyball to the person at the plate, who kicks the ball instead of batting it.

SPECIAL DAYS / ORDINARY DAYS

INSTEAD OF TV

Tonight instead of watching TV, try doing one of the following together as a family:

- Model objects out of clay. (You may make your own. See page 85.)

- Make collages of seeds, grains, cereal, paper scraps.

- Take a walk (maybe a drive to the woods or park before dark).

- Play badminton.

- Sing old songs.

- Have an everybody-do-something talent show.

- Have a puppet show.

- Have a read-aloud (each person gets to read or have his/her favorite poem or story read).

- Light candles and play old records.

- Catch fireflies.

- Have devotions outdoors on a porch, deck, patio, or sunroof.

- Have a bonfire (if open fires are allowed in your area) and roast marshmallows. If fires aren't allowed, roast them over the barbecue grill.

- Redecorate all the bulletin boards in the house. (Choose teams for each board.)

- Make Valentines (or Christmas cards, wrapping paper, etc.).

- Make popcorn balls.

- Do needlework, latch-hook rugs, macramé, etc.

- Play Twister, Trivial Pursuit, Ping-Pong, pick-up-sticks, jacks. (Dad, too!)

- String cranberries, popcorn, Cheerios, Lifesavers.

RECIPES FOR FUN

Simple crafts to do at home provide marvelous opportunities for children to develop creativity while at the same time enjoying the togetherness of working with Mom or Dad or an older brother or sister.

HOMEMADE PASTE

> **1 cup flour**
> **$^1\!/_2$ cup water**

Combine and mix until creamy. Store in covered container. This paste can be used for paper crafts or papier-mâché.

HOMEMADE FINGER PAINT

Mix equal parts of paste (made from recipe above) and liquid detergent and add food coloring. Or, add food coloring to liquid starch.

HINT: The best paper to use for finger painting is shelf paper, shiny banquet-table paper, or butcher paper. Paper should be dipped in water before applying paint. Try finger painting with toes, elbows, knees, fists, bits of sponge. (Chocolate pudding also makes great finger paint . . . and it's okay to taste the paint!)

YARN ART "STAINED GLASS"

- Cut several lengths (12–24 inches) of brightly colored yarn.

- Cover table or counter area with newspapers.

- Mix in a bowl:

> **2 tbsp. white glue**
> **2 tbsp. water**

- Soak the yarn in the glue; then squeeze through fingers to remove excess glue.

- Press yarn pieces to brightly colored tissue paper, creating the desired design.

- Allow to dry thoroughly.

- Trim tissue from edges.

- Hang the designs in front of a window or use shapes to create a mobile. Seasonal shapes may be made if desired.

CORNSTARCH AND SODA CLAY

This clay can be molded into shapes and vessels, or rolled on waxed paper and cut with cookie cutters. When dry, it can be painted.

NOTE: This mixture is NOT to be eaten, but is intended for crafts only.

Ingredients:

> **2 cups baking soda**
> **1 cup cornstarch**
> **$1^1\!/_4$ cups cold water**

- Combine all ingredients in saucepan until smooth.

- Bring to boil and boil one minute, stirring until clay is the consistency of mashed potatoes.

- Pour out onto a tray and cover with damp cloth until cool.

- Knead lightly (knead in a few drops of food coloring, if desired).

- Use immediately or store, wrapped airtight, in refrigerator. Warm to room temperature before using.

SPECIAL DAYS / ORDINARY DAYS

SPIN A LITTLE LOVE

- Have the family sit in a circle on the floor of the family room or den.

- Take turns spinning a bottle and telling something positive about the family member to whom the bottle points. Express the love message directly to the person rather than to the entire group.

- Go around the circle one more time and share events, surprises, or matters of interest that happened on that day.

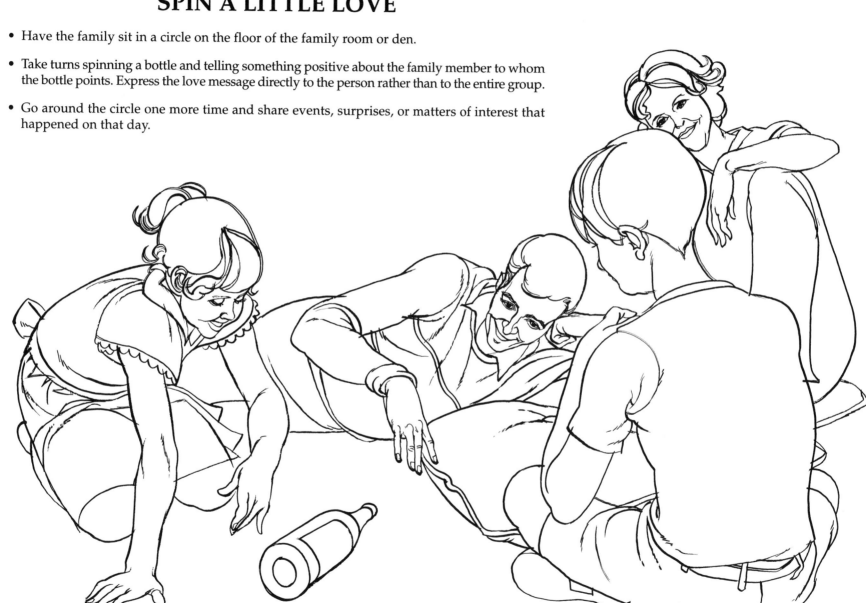

FOR A SPECIAL PERSON

A BREAKFAST DATE

- Choose one person in the family at a time for an early breakfast date.

- Include each child and your wife or husband.

- Let the date choose the place, or surprise him or her with some little nook you've lately discovered.

- Get up and leave early enough so that there is time to enjoy the dawn and eat and talk without a great deal of rushing.

- If it is a Saturday date, perhaps this would be a good chance to visit an elderly relative afterward. Give your child the gift of real friendship with people of *all* ages.

HONOR PLATE

- Choose an unusual or attractively colored plate to be used *only* on a special occasion.*

- Serve a meal on that plate when a member of the family is to be honored, such as on Father's Day, Mother's Day, a birthday, after receiving a good report card or an award, or after a difficult job is finished, etc.

- The honor plate is then washed and put away until the next "celebration" day.

HONOR FLAG

- Let each child design his or her own flag and then help in its creation.

- Fly the flag on any special day for that individual when the honor plate is being used.

FLAG OF HONOR

* For information on how to order a unique "You're Something Special" plate, see page 224.

SPECIAL DAYS / ORDINARY DAYS

THE DINNER HOUR

Try to make dinner a special occasion every day, even if you have small children. Try to include the following every evening:

- A centerpiece on the table. (This can be live or dried flowers, a basket of vegetables, a few stones and a piece of driftwood, a small limb of colorful leaves; anything that brings nature to the table.)

- Candles, lighted!

- Place-settings with napkins and real dishes—never paper.

Just as important as the physical setting is the pleasantness of the mealtime. Try to observe the following ground rules:

- Food that is nutritious, balanced, colorful, and delicious. (Even simple meals can be served with pizzazz!)

- Good conversation about the day from each person and encouragement offered from all.

- Soft music that is soothing to the nerves.

- No disciplining or heavy correcting of children.

- No fighting, whining, yelling, etc.

- "No-knock policy" is in effect for the thirty to forty-five minutes of mealtime. Nobody can say anything (even sarcastically or jokingly) to hurt another family member.

- No answering the telephone.

PUZZLE PLACE

When things are rushed or hectic, or when there are a lot of guests in and out, set out a huge 500-piece puzzle on the coffee table or game table

- Don't worry about the clutter. Just leave the puzzle out.

- Don't be surprised if guests who might otherwise be timid are drawn to the puzzle.

- Watch how many good conversations are precipitated by this simple-to-share task.

- Don't be surprised if kids are the best puzzle-solvers!

TAKE NOTE

Get into the habit of writing notes to persons in the family. A memo board in the kitchen is a good place to write notes, or:

- Put a note in a child's or father's lunch box.

- Slip a note in a geometry book or flute case.

- Leave a note on the mirror Dad will use when he shaves.

- Tie a note to the steering wheel of the car, truck, or tractor.

- Pin a note to the pillow when making the bed.

- Put a note on each person's plate before the dinner hour.

A note is a good way to say:

- "I'm glad I have you for a sister."

- "Thanks for always fixing such yummy meals."

- "Have a good day! I'll be praying for you during your math test."

- "As you drive to work, whistle, 'I Am Loved.'"

- "I just thought of five things I'm thankful for, and they all live in this house!"

Save special notes you've received. What a treasure they will be someday!

MAKING MEMORIES THROUGH THE SEASONS

SEASONS / SPRING

THE SPRING RUSH

Before spring actually arrives, watch for its promises. When the snow is still on the ground in late February or early March:

- Pick limbs of pussy willows and bring them inside. Put them in water and watch spring pop out!

- Pick forsythia at the first sign of budding, and bring it in.

- Plant tulip, daffodil, or hyacinth bulbs inside. Keep them watered and in a sunny window.

- Fill the house with construction-paper daisies. Tape them to windows, doors, refrigerator, or hang them with black thread from ceiling lights, etc.

- Welcome the birds with suet, tiny balls of meat, and seeds.

- Cut off the tops of milk cartons. Fill the cartons with soil and plant dwarf marigold seeds. They come up and grow quickly, and they may even be ready to bloom by the time it's warm enough to transplant them outside.

SPRING FIRSTS

Use a bulletin board or chalkboard in a prominent place to record spring firsts.

- Print or use cutout letters to create the title "SPRING FIRSTS" at the top of the board (or make a banner heading using computer graphics software).

- As a family, discuss the things that remind each person of a typical spring sight. Then decide on the things everyone should be on the lookout for and list them under the title on the board.

- The first person to spot a first sign of spring gets to put his or her name on the board beside the appropriate spring first, along with a picture of what was observed.

FIRST ROBIN CONTEST

Make a separate, yearly contest of any one of the ideas from the Spring Firsts above.

- After a cold eastern or midwestern winter, it's especially appealing to welcome spring by having a "first robin" contest. The first member of the family to see and report a robin is the winner.

- This contest can continue even after children are grown. No matter where they are, they can call home with "first robin" and claim the victory. This tradition represents the triumphant return of spring.

SPRINGTIME FUN

Here are two activities that are especially good for elementary and preschool aged children. But be prepared to have their older brothers and sisters want to join in too!

SPRING PENNY WALK

When the flowers and trees begin to bloom, take a "Spring Penny Walk" to enjoy the beautiful sights of spring.

- Toss a penny at each intersection to determine what path will be taken on the tour. Heads indicates a right turn and tails specifies a left turn. Enjoy the excitement of finding where "luck" takes you.

- After arriving back home, have each member of the family color a picture of what he or she likes best about spring.

- Share the pictures at dinnertime.

VEGETABLE POT GARDEN

Children love to eat what they grow.

- Put each child's name on a pot along with the name of the vegetable he or she will plant in it.

- Fill the pots with rich soil and plant a few vegetable seeds, such as carrots, radishes, or beans. Watching it grow from a tiny seed is fascinating for a young child.

- When the vegetable is harvested and prepared, put the child's name on the serving dish that contains it: Jim's Corn, Sherrie's Tomatoes, Nancy's Carrots.

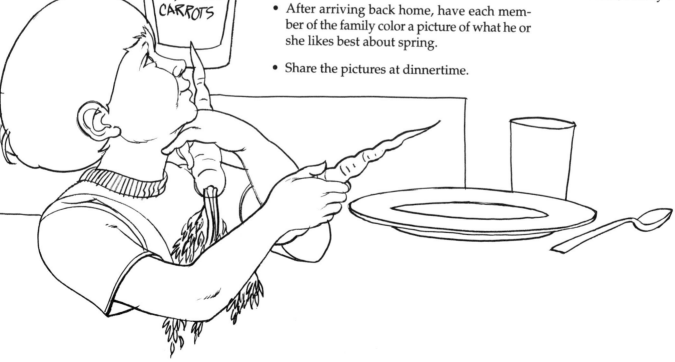

CHRISTOPHER'S CARROTS

BLOSSOM FESTIVAL

When the fruit blossoms first appear, have a family blossom festival. The following activities might be included:

- Decorate windows and bulletin boards with pictures drawn or cut from magazines (seed catalogs and garden magazines are best) of the fruit that is most commonly grown in your area: apple, peach, orange, cherry.

- Bring in dead limbs and decorate them with mock blossoms made from tissue or crepe paper.

- Make ice cream using frozen fruit from last year's crop.

- Celebrate the bees. Point out that without them there would be no fruit. Ask one child to find out why, and make a report at the supper table.

- Tie big "welcome ribbons" around each budding tree in the color of the fruit that the tree will bear. For example, use red or burgundy ribbons for cherries, peach for peaches, and gold for pears.

- Make garlands for the girls to wear on their heads. These can be made of floral wire or craft chenille wire (or pipe cleaners), tissue blossoms, and leaves.

- Plant a seedling together. If your yard is small, a dwarf tree is best. For specific instructions, see page 155. You may want to use this idea in the fall to allow time for the seedling to develop a root system during the dormant winter months.

SEASONS / SPRING

MAY DAY MORNING SURPRISE

- On May 1, get up before anyone else in the family.

- Go outside and pick a bouquet of spring flowers (daffodils, tulips, or whatever is in bloom in your area).

- Put them in a pretty basket that can hang on a doorknob. If you like, make your own basket from the instructions below.

- Go to the house of someone you want to surprise. Hang the May basket on the knob of the front door. Ring the doorbell and then hide behind the shrubbery or around the corner of the house.

- When someone comes to the door, jump out and yell, "May Day!"

MAY DAY BASKET

- Fold a sheet of construction paper diagonally.

- Cut off the bottom of the sheet to form a square. Save this piece to make a handle.

- Roll and glue side and bottom edges to form a cone shape.

- Cut two strips from the discarded piece and glue them together. Then glue one end of the long strip to each side of the cone to form a handle.

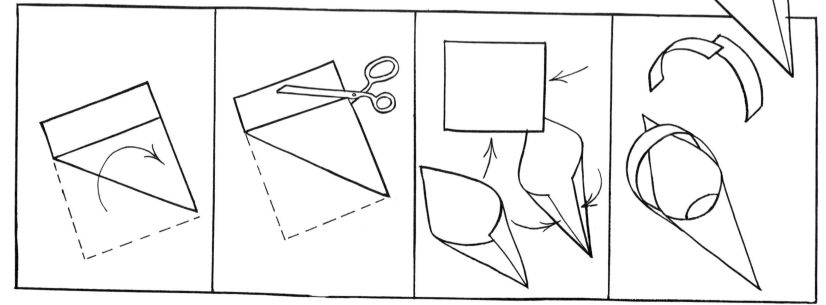

LAST DAY OF SCHOOL

Make it a tradition to do something special for the last day of school, such as:

- Go out for breakfast as soon as report cards have been picked up.

- Have the season's first bike hike.

- Tie "Welcome Summer" streamers across the doorway.

- Go swimming. Have a pool-opening party or go to the nearest public swimming pool.

- Buy some sandals.

- Celebrate the last day of school and the beginning of summer with *special* cookies (see Summer Lollipop Cookies described next) and lemonade.

SUMMER LOLLIPOP COOKIES

- Use a favorite crispy cookie recipe.

- Roll out the dough (not too thin) and cut it into round shapes with a cookie cutter or glass.

- Place the cookies on a baking sheet and insert a wooden popsicle stick one or two inches into the base of each circle.

- After baking, and after the cookies have cooled, frost them with a sunshine-yellow icing.

- Let each cookie represent the summer sun. Candies or raisins can be used to decorate the "sun" with creative faces.

- Serve with iced lemonade.

SEASONS / SUMMER

SEASONS / SUMMER

SUMMER MEMORY BOOK

MATERIALS NEEDED

Large spiral notebook or scrapbook
Paper
Marker pens or crayons
Glue
Adhesive tape
Measuring tape
Scales for weighing

- Starting at the beginning of summer, record dates of special outings, family activities, unusual events, etc. Paste or tape into the notebook ticket stubs, programs, place cards or other souvenirs that will fit into the notebook.

- Record the height and weight of each member of the family.

- At the end of the season look back on the activities of the summer and enjoy the memories you have created.

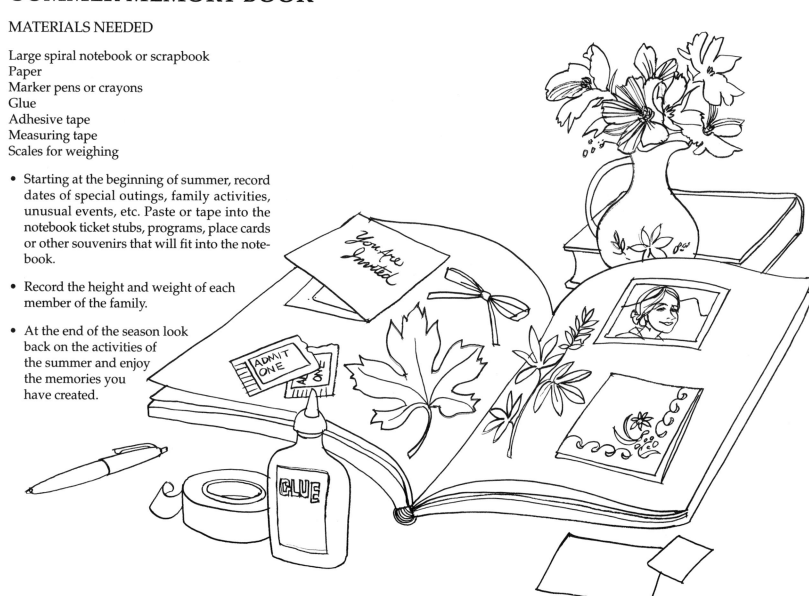

SUMMER EXCURSIONS

BEACH DAY

Throughout the summer, select one day each week—preferably the same day—for a family outing. Take the children to the beach, on a picnic, or on some other outdoor activity. Keeping this a regularly scheduled time will give the children something to look forward to and count on as their special time. Try not to combine this time with business or other social engagements, but keep it as a time for family only.

BERRY PICKING

Go as a family to pick berries together. The following checklist might be helpful:

- Be sure to wear clothing to cover arms and legs; blackberry and raspberry bushes are prickly.

- Take containers for each person.

- Choose old, comfortable clothes and shoes.

- Adults or older children might share some of their berries with the smaller persons. It's more fun when it "looks like ya got more."

- Plan something special afterward, like eating ice cream cones or drinking ice-cold lemonade.

- Have everyone help with the stemming and cleaning when you get home. Somehow, cooperation makes the berries taste even better.

- Freeze the berries you are not going to use right away. They can be frozen without sugar. Spread the washed, drained berries on a cookie sheet, and place it directly onto a shelf in the freezer. After the berries are frozen, scoop them into storage bags and return them to the freezer.

BICYCLE BREAKFAST

- Assemble the whole family early on a summer morning around six o'clock.

- Pack a simple breakfast that can be carried in bike baskets:

  individual cereals
  plastic spoons
  thermos of milk (or unopened cartons)
  thermos of coffee
  plastic bag of fruit (e.g., apple, orange and pineapple slices, grapes, raisins)
  plastic bag of bran or fruit muffins
  blanket or plastic tablecloth
  small Bible (eternal nourishment)

- Ride to the country on bikes. Get permission ahead of time to visit someone's woods, or go to the park or beach.

- Spread the blanket or tablecloth to sit on. Take time to comment on lovely things; keep conversation happy, observant, and thoughtful.

- Read together a short psalm of praise.

- After breakfast, let the children gather wild flowers or just run and play.

SEASONS / SUMMER

SEASONS / SUMMER

GALLERY THREE

- Gather together all of the crafts and similar items the family has made throughout the summer:

    jewelry
    rock sculpture
    yarn art
    collages
    paintings

- Make some lemonade and brownies.

- Sell your treasures at a "roadside" stand or a neighborhood craft sale.

- To make the project more meaningful, plan to donate some of the proceeds to homeless refugees from the Third World, a community relief project, or a family who recently lost their home in a fire, etc.

NEIGHBORHOOD ART SHOW

AHEAD OF TIME

- Agree on a place, time, and Saturday date for the art show with other families in the neighborhood. Give two or three weeks' notice.

- Make colorful signs about the event and post them on kitchen bulletin boards, fence posts, garage doors, and other places where they will attract attention.

- While all the children make art pieces for the show, the mothers or fathers can plan simple refreshments.

  NOTE: Any art can be entered: crayon drawings, paintings, clay sculpture, macramé, rock people, etc.

EARLY ON THE DAY OF THE EVENT

- Collect all entries at an early hour that has been announced in advance (e.g., 9:00 A.M.).

- Make sure each item is clearly marked with the name of the artist who created it.

- Separate entries into categories such as paintings, sculpture, drawings, etc.

- Set up displays, keeping categories together and arranging all entries so they may be clearly seen.

SHOW TIME

- Serve refreshments while parents and friends browse.

- Provide a cashier's table where art may be purchased for nickels, dimes, and quarters. Decide how money earned will be used. If it is to go to individual artists, have cashier keep track of items sold so money can be turned over to them when the show is over.

AFTERWARD

- Make each artist responsible for picking up all unsold items and taking them home.

- Have a clean-up committee ready to put away tables and chairs, pick up trash, and see that leftover refreshments are properly taken care of.

SEASONS / SUMMER

BACKYARD CIRCUS

AHEAD OF TIME

- Pick a Saturday to have a circus, and choose a place to hold it.

- Invite the neighborhood children to plan circus acts.

- Invite parents, grandparents, and friends to come and be the audience.

- On the day of the circus, set up folding chairs and make small sacks of popcorn and a pitcher of cold lemonade.

YOUR CIRCUS MIGHT INCLUDE

- Clowns

- A trapeze artist doing tricks on a swing set

- A strong man lifting fake barbells or a cardboard box with "1000 lbs." written on it

- A pet parade

- An acrobat

- A dog show with dogs jumping through hoops, performing obedience tricks, etc.

- A balancing act on a balance beam or on a board placed over a sturdy child's pool filled with water

BACKYARD MINIATURE GOLF

For a special party or just for fun, set up a miniature "golf" course in the backyard. Instead of golf equipment, use croquet mallets and balls to play the course.

- Make flags to mark each hole out of small dowel sticks and construction paper or bright plastic. (A plastic disposable picnic tablecloth is an inexpensive and readily available resource.) Number the flags with a broad-tipped felt-tip pen or marker.

- Make a gravel or sand trap by putting down plastic sheeting and covering it with sand or small rocks from the driveway. (Pick up and replace later.)

- Use old boards and a brick, log, or cement block to make an incline to go up and over.

- From half of a hollow piece of log (or an empty, large-size round oatmeal carton), make a tunnel to go through.

- Make an obstacle course from old paint cans set in rows.

- Use an old piece of guttering as a trough to go through. Drive small stakes on each side to hold it upright.

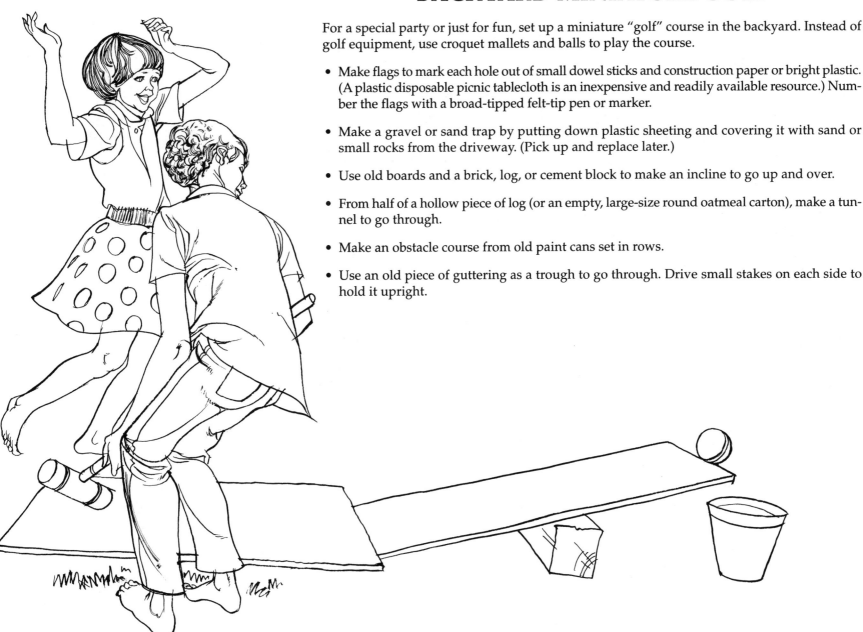

ONE-PITCH SOFTBALL

This yard game is good when there are not enough players for full teams. It is a game without losers and scoring is kept only to measure length of play (as "we play until 20 runs are scored").

• Beginning with batter and pitcher, put a player at each position, using as many positions as you have players available.

• The pitcher throws one pitch (his best try) and the batter must try to hit it. If he misses he is out. If he hits it, he runs.

• After this play all positions rotate. The pitcher becomes batter, batter (if he is out) goes to the outfield or third base, third baseman to second, second to first, and first becomes pitcher. If the original batter is on base, he tries to progress around the bases as new batters hit the ball. When he is "home" he takes his place in the rotation. As players successively fill the bases, there will be fewer defensive players and runners will find it easier to score. Enjoy!

• If there is a home run scored, that batter gets to bat again and no one rotates that round.

• When the score reaches the number originally agreed upon, the game is over.

THE SILENCE

Stillness is more audible than any sound, not tinny like so many sounds I hear these days.

The silence is full and rich, insistent . . . demanding that I listen and suggesting always that I'd be foolish not to. Only fools refuse the counsel of the wise, and this silence seems to know everything. It seems I've been a prodigal, traipsing along behind the band just like a thoughtless gypsy anywhere the living was easy, stealing morsels when I could have had the loaf.

Maybe it's the oaks and beeches. These oaks have housed a thousand generations of owls and jays, and have withstood abuse from countless woodpeckers and men. They've seen the fleet-footed native children tossing pebbles at their roots and chasing little fawns around between them. They've stood and heard the council casting lots for war or peace while fragrant pipe smoke wafted through their branches.

Perhaps it is the brook, whispering of its secret travels, nurturing the earth along its way, or maybe it's the earth, the pregnant fertile earth, pulling me like influential kin back to my moorings and my heritage.

The earth is calling me home to the simple and eternal things. It persistently calls me to reject the glitter of the transient and return to Father's house.

The silence—a voice asking one pointed and unavoidable question: will I return and inherit the earth? And here in the silence, the only sound to be heard is the whisper of my own answer.

SCHOOL DAYS

BACK-TO-SCHOOL SHOPPING SPREE

Make an "event" of shopping for back-to-school wardrobes. Spend some special time with each child alone.

- Go over last year's clothes; try everything on to see what still fits.

- Assess what may be handed down from an older brother or sister.

- Make a list of things needed to make the left-over wardrobe usable. List colors that are needed in accessories such as socks or belts.

- Make a realistic budget from the resources that are available. Explain the budget to the children. They will be more pleasant about "limitations" if they understand the budget and feel the parent is truly anxious to help.

- Plan a happy time looking for new things.

- Enjoy each other.

FIRST DAY OF SCHOOL

Make a special event of the first day of school. Try one or more of the following ideas, or create a tradition of your own:

- Wear one thing new.

- Take a picture to remember the day by.

- Go as a family to buy pencils, notebooks, and art supplies.

- Have a special "Celebrate Fall" supper of:

  chili
  vegetable sticks
  cheese slices
  assorted crackers
  homemade oatmeal cookies
  milk

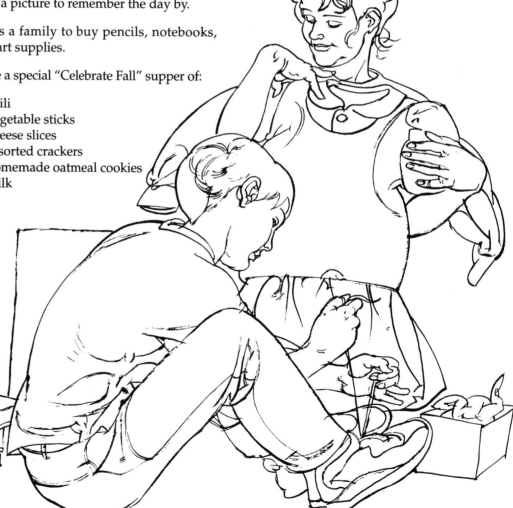

CRAYON-LEAF TRANSFERS

MATERIALS NEEDED

White or light-colored construction paper
Crayons
Iron

- Collect strong leaves without holes or flaws. Green leaves are usually stronger and not so easily torn.

- With bright crayons, carefully color the back side of the leaves. You may color a leaf all one color, or shade in several colors.

- Lay the construction paper on an ironing board. Arrange the leaves on top with the colored side toward the paper.

- Iron the leaves with a medium to hot iron. You may iron through a sheet of waxed paper if you prefer not to iron directly onto the leaves.

- Remove the waxed paper and leaves. A crayoned print will be left on the construction paper.

- Decorate a wall, bulletin board, or bedroom door with these bright art pieces.

NOTE: This idea can be used to make personal stationery, note cards, or wrapping paper.

SEASONS / AUTUMN

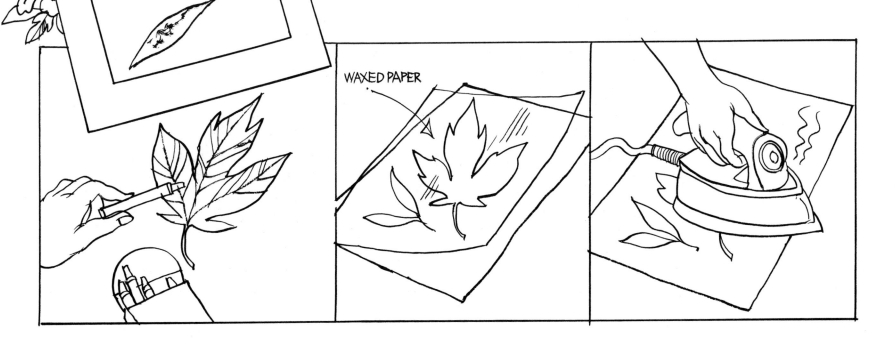

WAXED PAPER

STAINED-GLASS LEAVES

MATERIALS NEEDED

Waxed paper
Construction paper
Glue
Scissors
Iron

- Collect brightly colored leaves of different sizes and shapes.

- Make two *identical* picture frames from two sheets of construction paper by cutting out the centers of the sheets. Cut a rectangle, square, oval, circle, or more ornate shape from the center of each sheet. The outer edge of the sheet can also be cut into whatever shape is desired for the frame.

- Cut a piece of waxed paper large enough so that, when it is folded double, it is larger than the cut-out center of the construction paper frame

- Place one or two leaves inside the folded waxed paper.

- Iron with a medium to hot iron until waxed paper layers are sealed to each other around leaves.

- Place the sealed sheet containing the leaf or leaves between the two matching construction paper frames and glue the edges of the frames together.

- Tape "stained-glass leaves" to windows or hang in front of windows from a thread.

NOTE: This activity can be adapted for spring wildflowers.

AUTUMN'S PROMISE OF SPRING

AHEAD OF TIME

Buy several dozen bulbs of various kinds like daffodil, tulip, hyacinth, crocus. Check with a local nursery, seed store, or county agent as to the best bulb-planting time in your area.

AT PLANTING TIME

- Wear warm jackets or sweatshirts, and protect your hands with garden gloves.

- Use shovels to dig up the area where bulbs are to be planted, turning over all the soil and breaking up clods of dirt; rake smooth.

  NOTE: Let even small children help with shovels of their own.

- Take a moment to look at the bulbs and marvel at the unlikely miracle of life hidden within them.

- Plant bulbs so that the pointed side is up, about twice as deep as the height of bulb being planted. In very cold climates, plant the bulbs even deeper.

  HINT: Check the package for predicted height of plant. Plant bulbs of tallest plants toward center of back of planting area, shorter plants toward outside or front. Leave 4 to 6 inches of space on all sides of each bulb.

- Cover entire plot with a layer of mulch, leaves, or peat moss.

- Celebrate the completed job with mugs of hot chocolate, cider, or herbal tea. Wait for a glorious spring!

AUTUMN FAVORITES

Certain foods and beverages just seem to belong to special seasons. These two recipes surely say "Autumn's here!" (Of course, they're also good any time the weather's crisp.)

PUMPKIN PIE

Mix together:

> 1½ **cups canned or freshly cooked and pureed pumpkin**
> 2 **eggs**
> 1 **cup sugar**
> ½ **tsp. each of salt, ginger, cinnamon, nutmeg**
> 1 **can condensed milk**
>
> 2 **8- or 9-inch unbaked pie shells**

Fill shells and bake for 10 minutes at 425 degrees. Reduce heat to 350 degrees and bake for 35–40 minutes or until center of pie seems to be set.

HOT SPICED CIDER

- Fill a large commericial-size percolator with cider.

- In percolator basket, place:

> 6 **sticks cinnamon**
> 8 **whole cloves**
> ½ **lemon, cut into thin slices**
> ¼ **cup honey**

- Perk as usual.

  OR: tie the spices in a piece of cheesecloth and simmer in a crock pot or stovetop pan.

- Serve hot with a cinnamon stick or lemon slice in each cup.

FIRST SNOW

- Make up a simple song or cheer to sing or yell together at the sight of the first snowflake.

- Decorate your home with paper snowflakes. Cut snowflakes from white paper and tape them on windows, doors, and blackboards. Make them by folding a piece of paper in half, then in half again three more times (four times altogether). Cut snips randomly from the corners and edges. Use your imagination, and no two will be alike. Unfold the paper and hang the snowflakes by black thread in doorways and from ceiling fixtures.

- Use the snowflake cutouts as stencils. Lay one or more stencil outlines on black paper and spray the cut-out areas with white or silver spray paint. The sheet may be displayed as a poster or you may want to cut out the spray-painted snowflakes and display them individually.

- Build "snowmen" and "snow forts" from marshmallows and toothpicks. Set them on a 9" x 11" piece of mirror and use the display for a table centerpiece.

- To make an unforgettable treat, try some snow ice cream from the following ingredients. Snow ice cream must be flavored to taste, so no proportions can be given. Just experiment until it is right. (It is unadvisable to make this recipe in areas of high pollution.)

SNOW ICE CREAM

> **Large pan or bowl full of clean, newly fallen snow**
>
> **Cream**
>
> **Vanilla**
>
> **Granulated sugar**

- Mix cream and vanilla together.

- Layer snow in a chilled bowl, sprinkling sugar on each layer.

- Fold flavored cream into snow. Don't let cream drain to the bottom, but keep tossing gently.

- Eat immediately, as soon as cream is frozen.

SEASONS / WINTER

SEASONS / WINTER

SNOWED-IN SUNDAY

If you live in an area where you are snowed in during the winter and you are unable to get out to church on Sunday morning, let the children plan a home worship service:

- Sing songs and hymns together using family talent (guitar, autoharp, piano, or other instruments) for accompaniment.

- Share prayer requests that affect and concern the whole family. (This might be a good time to talk about school problems or family concerns and needs.)

- Let each person tell the things for which he or she is thankful.

- Include a time of prayer. Let one child choose two or three persons to pray.

- Let the children plan and give the devotional thoughts. (Don't be surprised if their "sermon" is as long as the one at church!)

- Be sure no one leaves the "service" without being told that he or she is *loved!*

A WARM BEAR HUG

Heading for a bed that's been warmed by his or her own special teddy bear can make bedtime an event your child will look forward to. Here is an idea for assuring him or her a "warm bear hug" on any cool night.

- Choose washable fake fur material to make a teddy bear hot water bottle holder. Use a remnant or buy the yardage suggested for the pattern you will use.

- Select a simple teddy bear sewing pattern, making sure it can be adjusted to fit around the hot water bottle you plan to use.

- Modify the body length so that the bottle just fits the opening and the neck of the bottle fits up into the bear's head.

- Insert a zipper in the back seam.

- Double stitch all the seams that intersect the zipper. Also double stitch the seams around the zipper itself.

- Stuff the arms, legs, and head with old nylons or poly-fill material.

- Fill the bear-bottle with hot water while the child is getting ready for bed, and tuck the cuddly animal between the sheets. Make sure it is not too hot for the child to touch.

- The bear will retain heat for several hours.

SEASONS / WINTER

TAFFY PULL

This special winter memory-maker is fun for all ages. Try it with a bunch of teenagers, two or three whole families, or three or four couples.

Here are some rules and ahead-of-time warnings:

- If you don't boil molasses long enough, it won't harden like it should as it is worked. (In this case, it will end up all over your hands, which is fun, too. Just eat it off!)

- Boiled down syrup is unmercifully hot! It quickly and severely burns anything it touches, so advise participants before starting that there will be no horsing around while syrup is being poured!

- If the taffy is to turn out white instead of sickly gray, hands that pull it must be very clean.

OLD-FASHIONED MOLASSES TAFFY

$2/3$ **cup molasses**
$1/3$ **cup light corn syrup**
$1\frac{1}{2}$ **cups firmly packed brown sugar**
$1\frac{1}{2}$ **tbsp. vinegar**
$1/2$ **cup water**
$1/4$ **tsp. salt**
•
$1/8$ **tsp. soda**
$1/4$ **cup butter**

Combine molasses, syrup, brown sugar, vinegar, water, and salt in large, heavy saucepan, stirring until sugar dissolves over low heat. Cook, stirring occasionally, until mixture reaches 265 degrees on candy thermometer. Remove from heat and stir in soda and butter. Pour into buttered large shallow pan and let cool until it can be handled—about 15 minutes. Turn edges in to center as it cools. Butter your fingertips; then cut off pieces of candy and pull and twist until candy changes color, to bronze. Twist in shapes or cut into 1-inch pieces with scissors dipped in cold water. Wrap in plastic paper. Makes 150 pieces.

NOTE FROM GLORIA: My grandma used to spread peanut butter on a flat strip of pulled taffy, roll peanut butter inside, seal edges, then snip off pieces with the scissors. These she wrapped in little pieces of waxed paper and twisted the ends to seal. I can just see her doing it!

WINTER GARDEN

While nothing is growing outside, start a garden inside. You can sprout the following vegetables in your kitchen window to add some color—and promise—to your winter days.

- Beans

    Fill sections of an egg carton or small paper cups with potting soil. Soak bean seeds or dried beans that have been purchased for cooking (navy beans, pinto beans, butter beans, etc.) in water overnight. Push two beans into the soil in each cup until they are just below the surface; then cover them. Water each day. When plants outgrow the cups or cartons, transplant them into clay flowerpots or coffee cans filled with potting soil.

- Carrots

    Cut off the tops of several carrots, leaving about one inch of carrot attached to top. Place carrot tops in a saucer or pie pan and add enough water to keep the bottom of each piece in water. Do not allow them to dry out. Before long, roots will form and new tops will grow.

- Sweet potatoes

    Cut sweet potatoes in the same way as carrots, and use the same method to grow green tops. Toothpicks can be inserted into vegetable pieces and used to support them from the rim of a small glass. Keep enough water in the glass that the bottom of the vegetable cutting stays submerged.

- Alfalfa sprouts or bean sprouts

    Fold several thicknesses of paper towel and place in the bottom of a flat bowl or large saucer. Soak the towel with water and sprinkle alfalfa seeds or beans on the soaked towels. Keep towels wet. In a few days the seeds will sprout and can be used in salads or on sandwiches. Sprouts can also be grown in a fruit jar. Put just enough water in the jar to partially cover the seeds. Put on the jar lid. As the water inside the jar evaporates, the air will become very humid, eventually condensing on the underside of the lid and "raining" down again on the seeds. The seeds will sprout within a few days, and a "garden" will grow inside your jar.

SEASONS / WINTER

BIRDSEED PRETZELS

Birdseed Pretzels are sure to draw a winter crowd of feathered guests. Explain to your children how difficult it is for birds to find enough to eat at this time of year and how much they can help by providing attractive food for them. To prepare Birdseed Pretzels:

- Cut a 12-inch piece of waxed paper and lay it flat on a protected surface. The corners may have to be taped down so the paper doesn't curl while the pretzels are being made.

- Squirt fairly wide lines (about 1/4 inch) of Elmer's Glue on the waxed paper to form a pretzel-like design in which all lines meet.

- Sprinkle bird seed or sunflower seeds to cover all the glue.

- Allow to dry overnight.

- Turn designs upside down on a flat surface and *carefully* peel away the waxed paper.

- Hang on limbs or fences with thread.

ANYTIME ACTIVITIES

THE FIRST TO SHARE

Celebrate the arrival of nature's first fruits by sharing as a family:

- The first lettuce from the garden.

- The first rose bud. Place it in a prominent place and enjoy its beauty together.

- The first apple from the tree. Divide it and make every bite count!

- The first cider. Go as a family to buy it. Make a tradition of it by always serving it some special way: with popcorn, hot with cinnamon sticks and honey, or straight from the jug.

- The first pumpkin pie. Make a tradition of inviting the same guest(s) to share it—a grandparent, friend, neighbor, or other relative.

DRAWING CONTEST

Plan a time for the family to be creative together. Drawing is a good outlet, and—who knows?—maybe you will find you have an artist in the family!

- Ask everyone in the family to draw a picture of what he or she thinks the present season would look like if it were a person. This can be done at the beginning of each new season. For example, ask, "If Spring were a person, what would he or she look like?"

- Have each person use color and detail to show what that season's personality and style seems to be.

- Sit in a circle and share the drawings with each other.

- Have each person explain why he or she pictures the season as he or she did.

- Thank God together for the uniqueness of each season.

POP SONGS

- You will need eight empty pop bottles, all the same size.

- Fill each one with a different level of water. (The more water, the higher the pitch that will sound when the bottle is struck.)

- Adjust the amounts of water in each bottle until you have the right amount to play the notes of a musical scale. Tap each bottle with a metal spoon to check its pitch.

- Let each family member have a turn playing a familiar melody or creating a new one.

SEASONS / ANY TIME OF YEAR

PARTY PUNCHBOARD

A punchboard is fun to use as a crazy game of chance at a party or other group gathering, or just for the family for after-supper fun. Traditional commercial punchboards are $1/2$" to $3/4$" thick boards in which holes have been made at regular intervals and then filled with rolled-up slips of paper containing printed messages. The holes are then covered over with paper. The person buying a turn at the punchboard then punches through the paper covering the hole he selects and extracts the printed message from it. A home version of the game can easily be made from inexpensive materials readily available in most households. You will need:

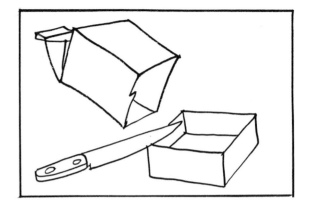

> an empty milk carton or a small, shallow jewelry box
> several sheets of plain paper
> several drinking straws, cut into $1/2$" lengths, or a supply of tiny rubber bands of the type
>   worn with dental braces

- Cut off the milk carton about 1" above the bottom; discard the top. Use the bottom portion as a shallow tray, or use the bottom or the lid of the jewelry box. This tray will hold the paper messages for the game.

- Cut the sheets of paper into strips approximately 1" wide and write a fun instruction on each strip. (See ideas below, but be prepared to use your imagination for the number of messages that you will need for filling the tray.)

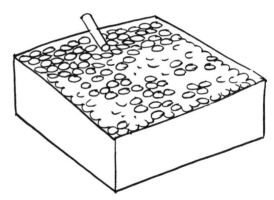

- Roll each strip tightly and stuff it into a section of paper straw tubing or secure it with a tiny rubber band.

- Stand the rolls on end in the tray or box. Make enough rolls to fill the tray completely.

- Play the game by having each person in turn poke a sharpened pencil into the center of a message-tube and pull it out. The player must then follow whatever instructions the message gives.

SAMPLE MESSAGES:

Try to touch your elbow with your tongue.
Trade socks with another person.
Pick up a Lifesaver on a toothpick held in your teeth and carry it across the room.
Teach the others a new aerobic exercise.
Teach the others a cheer you learned in school.
Tell what three books you would take to a desert island.
Tell one thing you like about each person present.
Run outside, touch your toes three times without bending your knees, and then skip back to
    the group.
Bark like a small, nervous dog.

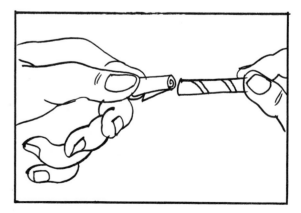

MAKING MEMORIES IN SPECIAL PLACES

SPECIAL PLACES / VACATIONS

GETTING READY FOR VACATION

VACATION TIME / ADVENTURE TIME

Make vacation time an adventure for the whole family. Here are some ideas for family discussion:

Take a cruise
Stay on a working farm
Take a backpacking expedition
Go white-water rafting
Stay at a real working western guest ranch
Participate in a cattle drive
Go mountaineering
Take a hiking vacation in the great northwest
Stay on an island
Learn to snorkel, ski, soar in a balloon,
     canoe, sail
Visit a country inn

For addresses, prices, and descriptions of ways and places to go on vacations like these, request a catalog or send for these books from The Berkshire Traveler Travel Shelf:

Adventure Travel
Country Inns and Back Roads
Farm, Ranch, Country Vacations

Berkshire Traveler Press
Stockbridge, MA 01262

DRAW A VACATION

Let the entire family help decide what kind of vacation to take this year.

- Obtain enough computer paper, brown wrapping paper, or shelf paper for the whole family to draw a wall mural. Choose a place to display it when it is finished; then measure off the amount of paper to fit the space that is available.

- After dinner, let each member of the family draw a favorite vacation or trip on his or her section of the mural. Use crayons, markers, pens, or paints.

- Discuss what everyone would like to do this year.

- Hang the finished product in the place that has been chosen for it. Seeing and talking about each person's ideas may help the family decide on a vacation that will be more fun for everyone.

VACATION SURVIVAL BAG

Pack a special duffel or tote bag with vacation craft supplies. Some "musts" are:

    a bag of plaster of Paris
    white glue
    string, yarn, or old shoestrings
    jackknife
    box of crayons
    box of colored chalk
    drawing paper
    pipe cleaners or chenille craft wires
    adhesive tape
    play dough (this is handy for making
        plaster of Paris molds)
    empty notebook for writing poems,
        memories, and vacation notes
    small plant press

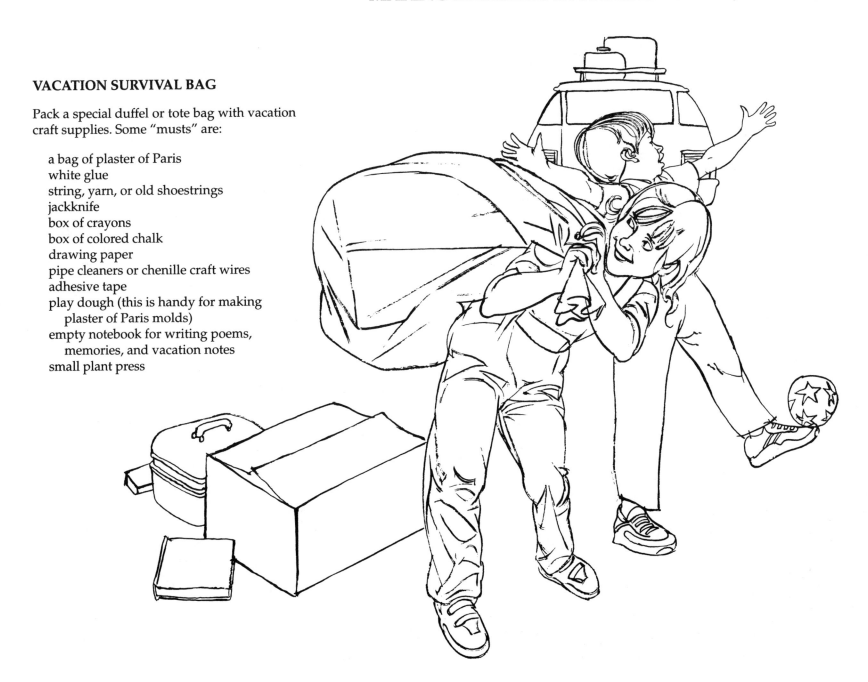

SPECIAL PLACES / VACATIONS

SPECIAL PLACES / VACATIONS

TRAVEL FUN

GOURMET TRAVELER

- Collect menus of all the restaurants enjoyed by the family while on the trip.

- Arrange them in an attractive grouping on a den wall or in a hallway. (Decorators often use this idea.)

- Other objects can be added to form an interesting display.

- Be creative.

MAP MATTERS

- On a traveling vacation, take along a map of the area you are going to visit.

- Have the children trace the route with a marking pen as you travel.

- Look on the map at what lies north, south, east and west of your route. Talk about the climate, terrain, agriculture, industry of the area, and interesting sights you see out the window of your car, plane, train, or bus.

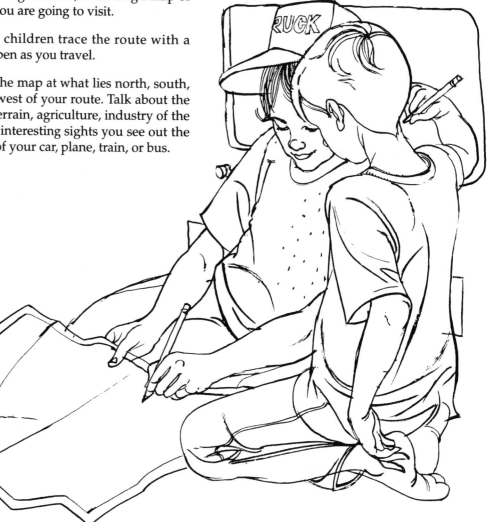

GAMES IN THE CAR

- Draw 2-inch squares on 4" x 6" cards. Before leaving on the trip, list in each square an object you may see on your journey such as a barn, horse, etc. Later, when you see the object listed on your card, call it out and mark it off. The first to finish his or her card is the winner.

- While the driver watches the odometer, each family member tries to guess when he or she thinks the car has gone one or five or ten miles. The one who is closest wins a point.

- The "Alphabet Game" is played with letters on road signs and businesses. The first person who gets through the alphabet wins. The winner gets to choose the restaurant for dinner.

- As a family project during a long journey, attempt to locate and record on paper at least one license plate number from all fifty states and the District of Columbia. (Some resort centers have dozens of cars from out of state.)

SPECIAL PLACES / VACATIONS

SPECIAL PLACES / VACATIONS

VACATION MEMENTOS

TREASURE TRIP

- Collect natural treasures on your trip such as sea shells, flowers, leaves, rocks, seed pods, deserted bird nests, pine cones, cocoons, pieces of wood. Where collecting is prohibited, take pictures of natural treasures.

- After the trip is over, display your collection of objects or pictures on a table or fireplace mantel, or glue them in an interesting design on heavy poster board.

- Discuss when, where, and how the treasures were found and in what locations, etc.

MEMORY COLLAGE

- Take along a bottle of white glue on your trip.

- Collect pieces of bark, driftwood, or flat rock to use as a base for your collage.

- If local regulations allow it, collect small objects from each picnic site, hike, boat trip, mountain climb, etc.

- Spend one evening (or rainy day) toward the end of the trip arranging the memory objects and gluing them to the base.

- On the back, write the place and date of your vacation. Attach a gummed hanger or wire to the back for hanging.

VACATION ANNUAL

- Buy a durable empty book at an art shop, novelty shop, or bookstore.

- Label the front cover "Vacation Book."

- Take it on each vacation and label a fresh section for each vacation, for example: "Grand Canyon, June 1992" or "Big Sur, June 1994."

- Draw pictures to depict the sorts of things you did on the trip.

- Have each person in the family, any guests, and anyone you meet and get to know write in the book. Share thoughts, special moments, funny incidents, poetry, etc. Be sure to have each person sign his or her name. Have the children include their ages.

- Save the book for the next vacation and begin a new section.

Reading over old entries can bring back lovely memories as well as bring a good laugh: "Look how Tommy wrote when he was three!" "Remember, Grandma went with us on that trip."

SPECIAL PLACES / VACATIONS

LATE SUMMER VACATION
BEAVER ISLAND, MICHIGAN

Curtain call to summer . . .

Seems as though the action should only just be starting.
School begins this week, but vacation holds us a few days longer for
    its own education.
Pines against the blue, blue sky;
White sails slithering between resting white gulls;
Quaint little buildings clustered along the northeast cove,
   huddled together the better to withstand the tides of
      both the water and the world—
   simple, practical structures, preserved and cared for but without
     trim and frills,
   painted white, mostly, to protect against wind and weather.

I will my mind's eye to memorize, imprint indelibly,
   images of our treasured time together.
Benjy and Amy, racing down the dunes,
   squealing and scooting on their bottoms to the water's edge;
Suzanne, sitting apart, piling sand,
   thinking, changing, turning, reluctant to let go of childhood.
What moments will they remember?

Ferry ride adventure in a simple, awkward tub of a boat,
   blunt, high, like Noah's ark.
      (We could be animals, hanging out from little corners of the
      deck, stormy water tossing us around like marbles in a cup,
      with not even a raven we can send to reconnoiter.)
Journey by a narrow road through the virgin timber
   to roast hot dogs beside a hidden lake.
Outrageous liquid crimson moon rising out of a satin sea,
   fresh from the moon-vat,
   dripping until suspended and attached to the black sandpaper sky.

Easy alliance of sausage and sunrise,
   mellowed by the aroma of hot coffee and comfortable relationships,
   shared in cottages warmed by itinerant children.
Bicycle rides to the village,
   past greedy gulls' feeding ground littered with man's castaways—
   mutilated T-bones, sardines, chicken bones, bread crusts
   (my apple coffeecake, too, toll for crossing to their side of the island)
   —but few shells, except for clams
      (only experts find good ones).
Icy little stream, numbing bare feet;
   beside its banks rocks, flat, shaved,
   perfect for skipping two, three, four times with practice.
      ("Everybody throw when I say three!
      One, two, three!")
Old abandoned car, almost hidden by weeds and scrub,
   wooden-spoked wheels and running board outlasting metal body.
Moss, a hundred kinds, plush, extravagant;
Indian peacepipes, smoked silently, unseen and uncensured;
Monarchs and bank swallows, flitting between my thoughts,
   smell of cedar overpowering my consciousness.
Loons, gulls, nightingales, human voices are stilled by insistent
      silence
   while the setting sun plays out its drama on this last night.

Too soon, the departing ferry's sharp announcement breaks the spell,
   and reminds of summer's end.
Leaving this quaint, quiet place, I rejoice
   that its peace and solitude are portable;
   that as we walk crowded streets,
      noisy school corridors,
      busy office building hallways,
      familiar stairways in our own bustling house,
   the tranquility given to our souls may remain.

SOIL DIARY

- Collect some small clean baby-food jars. (If you don't have a baby, ask someone who does to save some jars for you.)

- On each vacation or out-of-state family outing, fill a jar with the soil from the place you visit.

- Label the sample with the date and place.

  NOTE: Plastic wrap under the lid will prevent moisture from rusting the lid.

- Display the collection on a shelf or mantel at home or in a summer cottage.

  SUGGESTION: Find out what is grown in the soil in each of the following areas and what conditions produced its color and texture, for example:

  Red Georgia clay
  Hawaiian black volcanic sand
  Wisconsin loam
  Michigan brown sand from Lake Huron
  White sand from Florida
  Orange (iron) soil from Copper Harbor, Michigan
  Volcanic dust (from Mount Saint Helens)
  Salt from Utah

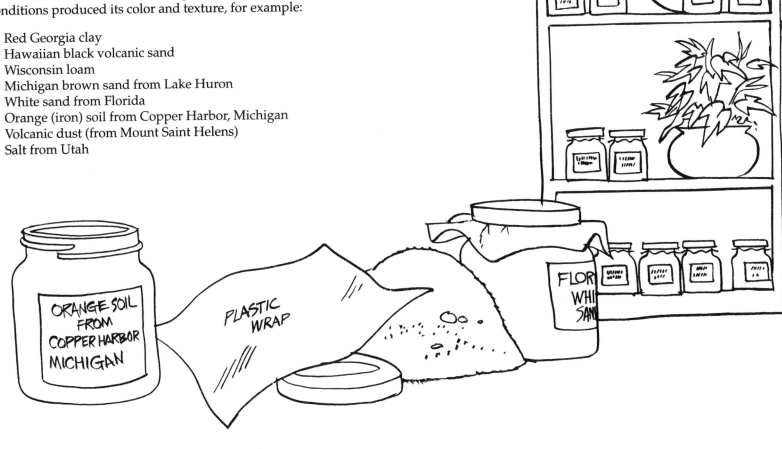

AN UNVACATION

When you are unable to take a vacation because of financial strain, time limitations, or other reason, here are some ideas that can be fun, interesting, and even educational:

- Attend a court session.

- Go to a museum.

- Visit the factories or large businesses in your area. Some may have regular tours.

- Go to an art gallery.

- Check out a book at the library to be read aloud to the whole family.

- Go to the park.

- Go to the beach.

- Attend a city council meeting.

- Watch for bargain sales at material stores and make back-to-school wardrobes. (This is a good time for daughters to learn how to sew.)

- Visit another church that has a different kind of worship service from your own church.

FOREST FOSSILS

MATERIALS NEEDED

Plaster of Paris
Plant press or two flat pieces of wood and a rock
Plastic-coated paper plate or foam plate

• Collect different kinds of leaves, blossoms, seeds, pods, and insects.

• Press the leaves and blossoms overnight in a plant press or between two pieces of wood weighted with a rock. A huge book will work, too. Be sure to put a layer of paper towel on each side of the leaves to keep moisture from damaging the pages of the book. This removes natural moisture from the leaves, which otherwise will curl when placed in the plaster of Paris or will fail to adhere to it permanently, if that is desired.

• Mix a small portion of plaster of Paris with enough water to make a mixture about the consistency of cake batter. Pour into a paper plate.

• Before the plaster hardens, press the specimens into the plaster until a definite imprint is made; then remove. You may remove the specimens or leave them embedded in plaster.

• As the plaster hardens, it will feel warm. After it cools completely and has set firmly, gently remove it from the plate. If you wish to hang your forest fossils, attach a large gummed hanger to the reverse side.

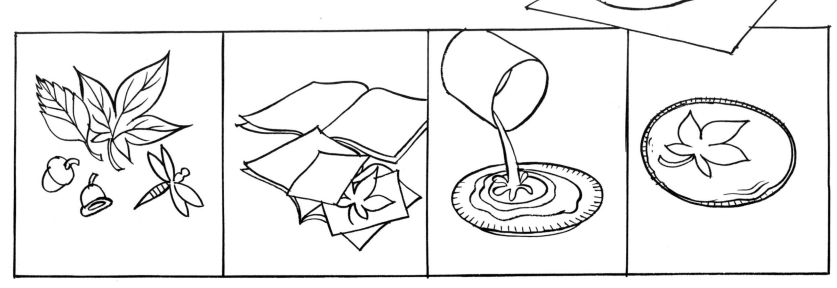

SPECIAL PLACES / WOODS

SPECIAL PLACES / WOODS

REMINDERS OF THE WOODS

WOODLAND RUBBINGS

MATERIALS NEEDED

Thin drawing or typing paper
Crayons or chalk

The woods are full of lovely textures. Find an interesting surface such as the back side of a leaf, the bark of a tree, a fossil rock, the rough cap of an acorn, the knobby surface of a hedge-apple, Osage orange, etc.

- Make a "rubbing" by placing paper over the textured surface and rubbing back and forth carefully with crayon or chalk. Like magic, the texture will be recorded on your paper.

- Label the texture, if you like, then display your woodland rubbing on the cabin door or paste it in your vacation scrapbook.

WOODLAND MOBILE

Where it is allowed, collect small specimens such as:

   bark
   algae or lichens
   dried weed pods
   large seeds
   pine cones
   pebbles from a brook-bed

When you get back to camp or home, tie woodland treasures to a clothes hanger with differing lengths of string, thread, or yarn. Hang it indoors or in a sheltered spot outdoors.

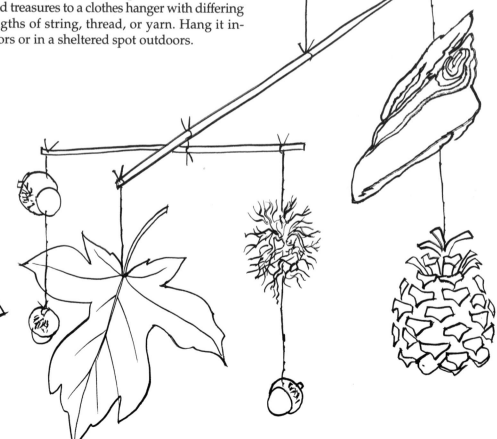

MACARONI JEWELS

MATERIALS NEEDED

Macaroni of different sizes
String, yarn, or shoestrings

Some rainy evening in camp, make jewelry by stringing all kinds of macaroni (any kind with a large hole) onto string or shoestrings.

HINT: Yarn can be made easy to thread by wrapping a piece of adhesive tape around one end or by dipping the end of the yarn in melted wax.

SPECIAL PLACES / WOODS

DIONIS BEACH

On the last night of a seaside vacation we had a wiener roast on the Dionis Beach. Then we searched the water for little creatures, and found dozens of hermit crabs and other kinds of sea life. This beach was certainly our favorite—quiet, so secretive and promising, so romantic. Benjy's, Amy's, and Suzanne's young profiles between the pink horizon and the quiet sea are frozen in my mind as if someone had stopped a movie projector to take a closer look at one frame—this frame—this moment. Benjy, so innocent on the outer edge of childhood—all freckled and wind-blown with his sun-bleached hair and dancing eyes, his sturdy little body and wide, strong hands. Amy, so straight and tall with her first "real hairdo"—excited, bubbling, expectant, and always optimistic, always making peace and making do with whatever circumstances or people she has to work with. Suzanne, poised on the path to womanhood, yet wise enough to keep her childhood's wide-eyed wonder and excitement over simple things—protective, inventive, and loyal, with an eye for art and beauty; self-sufficient, yet needing to be loved and touched and protected, too.

Even today, years later, I can see their faces there between the sea and sky. Barely children they were, yet hardly mature. I remember standing on tiptoe and trying to hold that moment in my mind, for that visit to our precious island would be like no other. We had celebrated many happy days of childhood on those beaches and watched the little footprints in the sand. That year we made the island our welcome mat for grown-up days. Looking closely down the beach I could see the prints of tiny toddler feet growing bigger as they ran along until they ended right in front of me, long and slim and almost the size of mine. Growing feet. Running feet. Feet I held in my hand and counted "piggies" on. Feet I scrubbed the mud and sand and grass stain from. Feet I tied sneakers on and guided into stiff, new Sunday shoes. Feet I taught to pedal bikes and to roller skate. Feet I taught to paddle when they swim and hold "just so" in stirrups when riding horses, with toes pointed in and heels out. Feet that learned to go where I couldn't follow . . . up tall trees, down school hallways, on dates. I watched those feet take first steps, toddle, walk, skip, balance, kick footballs, run bases, march in parades, and dance pirouettes. And at every stage I watched them leave the current footwear behind to run barefoot and free down those beloved beaches.

FOOTPRINTS IN TIME

As your children grow, you may often wish you could "hang onto them" just the way they are at that moment. Permanent "footprints" made from year to year serve to fill that yearning and at the same time make an interesting record of each child's growth.

- Pack a plastic bag full of plaster of Paris in your suitcase.

- At the beach, mix the plaster and the required amount of water (fresh water—salt water will not set).

- Have each child make a clear, deep footprint in damp sand.

- Pour the print full of plaster.

- Let the plaster stand until it is semi-soft. Then insert a bent hair pin into the plaster for a hanger.

- When the plaster cast is cool and hard, dig away the sand and remove the "footprint."

- On the back of each footprint, write the person's name, age, and the place where the footprint was made.

- Repeat each year, and keep a collection on a special wall or in each child's room.

SAND CASTLES

It is great fun for the whole family to work together to build a sand kingdom, using wet sand and various molds such as sand buckets, empty coffee cans, cottage cheese and yogurt cartons, or clean soup cans.

Try a more fantastic sculpture by building close enough to the ocean to dig a small pit that fills up with water. Now, take dripping wet handfuls of sand from the pit and drizzle them in mounds away from the pit. As soon as the drippings hit the ground they will drain, leaving beautiful sculptured peaks. These castles can have dozens of pencil thin towers and spires.

Now add sticks and bits of tissue for flags, use fingers to drill tunnels, and make moats to protect your kingdom. (Be sure to throw away any bits of trash when you are finished.)

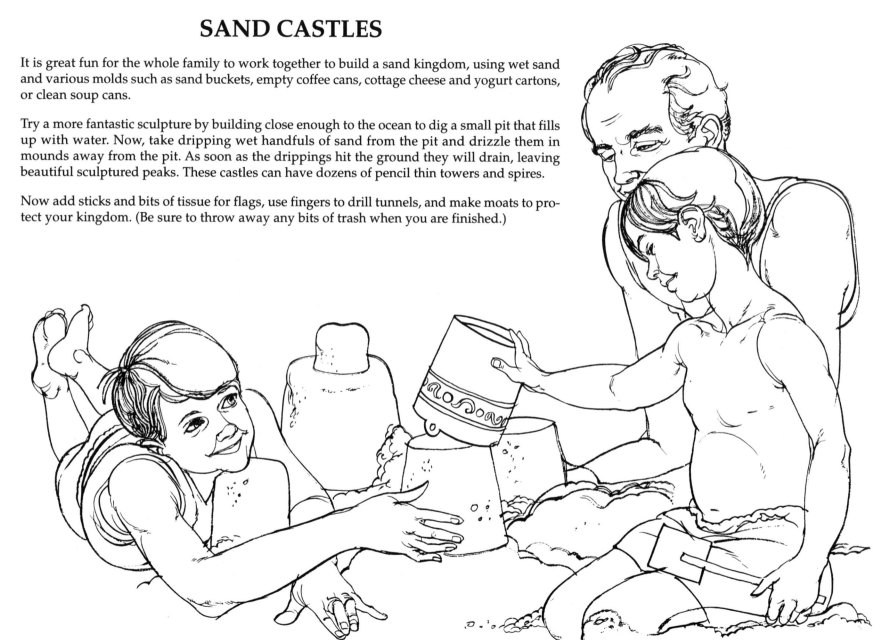

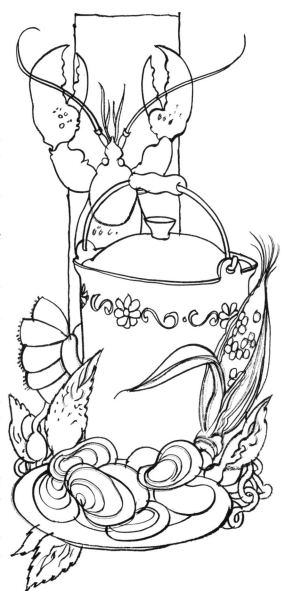

CLAMBAKE

AHEAD OF TIME

Choose a beach location for your clambake and check for permission to build a fire there. Gather the supplies and cooking utensils you will need.

MATERIALS NEEDED

A clam boiler or large enameled pot with lid
A pailful of fresh water
Lots of seaweed
One baking potato for each person (wrap potatoes in foil)
One or two pieces of uncooked chicken, per person, each piece wrapped in cheesecloth
One lobster for each person
One ear of corn per person. Leave corn in husks, then wrap in foil
Plenty of steamer clams
Melted butter

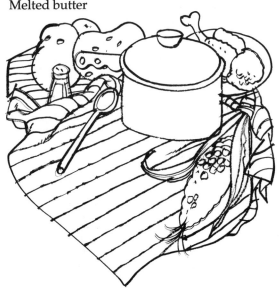

AT THE BEACH

- Obtain a list of beaches where fires are permitted and, if necessary, get the required permit to build one.

- Dig a small pit, and lay a charcoal and wood fire.

- Dig clams; then scrub them with a brush and soak them in a pail of fresh water for an hour or more.

- Rinse the seaweed several times in clean water; then soak for an hour to get rid of sand.

- Line bottom of clam pot with a 4-inch layer of seaweed and add one quart of fresh water.

- Put pot over hot fire until water boils. Then add wrapped potatoes and more seaweed. Cover with lid and cook for fifteen minutes on lower fire.

- Add chicken and more clean seaweed. Cover and wait fifteen more minutes.

- Add lobsters and more seaweed. Cover again and cook five more minutes before adding corn. Cook ten minutes more.

- Add clams now and steam until clams pop open (about ten minutes). All the cooking will take about an hour. Melted butter can be served in clam shells.

- Be sure to have lots of paper napkins handy because this meal will be messy, but delicious and great fun!

SPECIAL PLACES / WATER'S EDGE

SEASIDE SOUVENIRS

SEA CHIMES

MATERIALS NEEDED

A small inexpensive wicker basket or wicker hot pad
String
Lots of shells that have holes through them

- Tie a string to the exact center of the hot pad or basket bottom, knotting the string securely so it will not pull through when the chimes are hung. At the free end of the string, make a loop for hanging the chimes.

- String shells in several lengths of string, tying knots to leave small spaces between the shells.

- Tie the strands of shells around the rim of the basket or hot pad.

- Hang the sea chimes in an open place, for example, from a porch ceiling or under a deck.

SEA JEWELRY

- Gather together an assortment of inexpensive baubles from the variety store such as:

  plastic hair combs
  wide plastic rings
  plain wide plastic bracelets

- You will also need:

  white glue
  tiny colorful shells
  tweezers

- Make tiny dots of white glue on the surface you'd like to decorate.

- With tweezers, place a tiny shell on each drop of glue. Continue until the comb, bracelet, or ring is beautifully decorated with seashore "jewels."

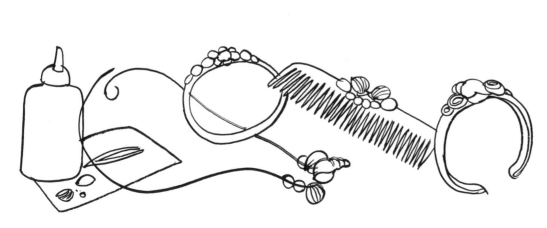

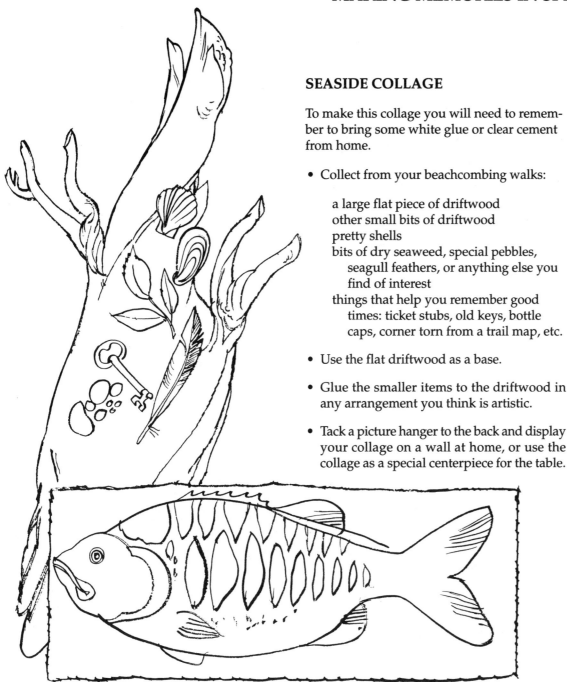

SEASIDE COLLAGE

To make this collage you will need to remember to bring some white glue or clear cement from home.

- Collect from your beachcombing walks:

  a large flat piece of driftwood
  other small bits of driftwood
  pretty shells
  bits of dry seaweed, special pebbles, seagull feathers, or anything else you find of interest
  things that help you remember good times: ticket stubs, old keys, bottle caps, corner torn from a trail map, etc.

- Use the flat driftwood as a base.

- Glue the smaller items to the driftwood in any arrangement you think is artistic.

- Tack a picture hanger to the back and display your collage on a wall at home, or use the collage as a special centerpiece for the table.

PRIZE PRINTS

To make Prize Prints, you will need to take along with you to the beach some India ink or tempera paint and a few squares of white muslin.

- Take your prize fish or favorite sea creature to a sandy place on the bank, *after* you have rinsed it off well.

- Dry it or let it dry.

- Paint one side of the fish with India ink or tempera paint.

- Cover the inked side of the fish with a piece of clean muslin. Gently press the cloth against the fish and rub the cloth with your hand, being careful not to scoot the cloth as you do so.

- Carefully lift the cloth.

- Wash the fish again; then go ahead and clean it up to cook for supper.

- Take the life-size print of your prize catch or find home with you and mount the print on a piece of plywood or fiberboard.

SPECIAL PLACES / WATER'S EDGE

SPECIAL PLACES / DESERT

DESERT TREASURES

DESERT SHADOW BOX

MATERIALS NEEDED

A sturdy box (gift box or sawed-off shoe box)
Poster board or heavy construction paper
Glue
Desert finds such as small stones, bones, dried cactus, seed pods, feathers, plaster castings of small animal footprints, etc. Note: In many parks and other natural areas visitors are not allowed to take anything out of the park. Be sure to check local regulations before beginning your collection.

- Make partitions in the box with strips of poster board the same width as the depth of the box.

- Cut the strips enough longer to allow you to bend each end to make a tab to be glued to box. "Windows" in your box may be symmetrical, or you may prefer to make them random sizes.

- If you like, spray paint the box before going on to the next step.

- Glue tiny treasures in each window, taking care to balance sizes and shapes artistically.

- When you get home, stand the box on end. Place a desert book and a candle alongside to make a lovely centerpiece or table display.

DESERT TREASURE STORAGE BOX

MATERIALS NEEDED

An egg carton
Pieces of contact paper or colorful stickers

Decorate the lid of an egg carton with desert designs, letters, or desert flowers cut from contact paper or with colorful stickers. Fill the carton with special desert finds.

DESERT IN A JAR

MATERIALS NEEDED

A clean, wide-mouthed half-gallon or gallon
   pickle jar with holes in the lid
Sand
Small desert rocks or dried broken bits of dead
   cactus
Small live cactus plants (never take cacti from
   the desert; buy them in desert stores)

• Pour about two inches of sand in the bottom
  of a clean jar. Plant cactus plants, being careful not to get prickles in your fingers. (Cotton
  garden gloves might make the job more
  pleasant.)

• Place a few colorful rocks or broken bits of
  dead cacti around the plants.

• Add a small amount of water, just enough to
  dampen the sand.

• Place the lid on the jar and put your desert
  garden in a sunny window.

SPECIAL PLACES / DESERT

SAND LAYERING

- Bring home a bag of sand from your vacation to do sand layering. You will need:

    sand
    a clear jar with lid (tall thin olive jars, short fat pimento jars, jelly jars, pickle jars, etc.)
    plastic cups (not foam cups)
    paper towels
    powdered fabric dyes or food coloring

- Set out as many plastic cups as you want colors of sand, and fill each cup half full of sand.

- In another cup, mix water and as much dye powder or drops of food coloring as it takes to make the color you want. Remember the dyed sand will be lighter than the colored water, so go a shade or two darker.

- Pour colored water into the cup of sand and stir with a plastic spoon.

- Rinse the water cup before repeating the coloring process with each new color of sand.

- When all the cups of sand have dye in them, let them stand at least fifteen minutes.

- Carefully drain the water off of the sand. (It's better to do this outside so that no grains of sand will go down the drain.)

- Cover a worktable or countertop with waxed paper; then lay out four sheets of paper towel (four thicknesses) for each color of sand. Spoon the sand onto paper towels, spread it out a bit, and let it dry. Keep colors separate.

- After the sand is dry, carefully begin to spoon it into dry jars in beautiful layers. You can make "mountains" and "valleys" by mounding sand of one color against the side of the jar, filling in the valleys with another color.

NOTE: This activity can also be enjoyed with purchased sandbox sand.

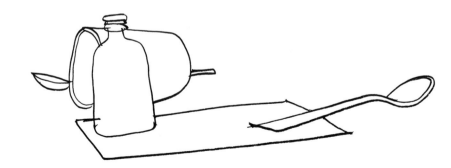

SAND PAINTINGS

MATERIALS NEEDED

Brightly colored chalk
Sand samples
Baby food jars or empty 35mm film containers
White glue
Manila paper or poster board

- Collect sand samples of different textures.

- Crush some brightly colored chalk with a rock or hammer and mix with sand to create desired colors. Or use dyes or food colors, as described on page 140.

- "Paint" your picture with glue, one item at a time.

- Then sprinkle colored sand on the glue. Tip picture gently to remove excess sand. Collect this sand on another piece of paper; then return unused colored sand to container.

- Keep adding glue and colored sand until your painting is finished.

HINT: If you first "paint" the background such as sky, sea, mountains, fields, and let this part dry for a few hours, you can add more detail (buds, trees, flowers, boats), even on top of the dried background.

SPECIAL PLACES / DESERT

ALTITUDE FOLIAGE DIARY

AHEAD OF TIME

Pack in your backpack some sort of book that can double as a devotional and a press for this project.

- If you are in an area where it is allowed, collect samples of foliage at each altitude. Place between book pages to preserve. Include with each sample a slip of paper identifying it by number according to the order in which it was collected. Make sure you don't "collect" poison ivy!

- In a diary, use corresponding numbers to describe the terrain of the elevation at which each sample was found.

- When you return to camp or home, mount each sample on a separate sheet of art paper or page of a scrapbook, and record any comments about what you experienced the day the sample was found and a description of the terrain or view.

- Protect the pages with a cover page on which you write your name, date, mountain area climbed, and state; or, glue a title page to the scrapbook that you have used.

- Keep it where your family can look through it often to recall happy memories.

MOVING ALERT

MOVING TO A NEW HOME

- Discuss with young children the things in the house that will be moved. Be sure they are assured that their beds, trucks, favorite stuffed animals, records, etc., will go along.

  NOTE: This is *not* a good time to sort out old toys, games, tennis shoes, etc. Neither should you change from crib to bed, do away with bedtime blanket or pacifier, or drastically change feeding habits.

- See that the whole family, including young children, is involved in the moving process. Even young children can neatly stack wash cloths, towels, or dish towels into a box or fill a container with stuffed toys, paper products, canned goods, utensils or lids, plastic ware, or books.

- When you arrive at the new place, assemble the children's rooms first and unpack their favorite things. Be sure the children are present for this even if they have to be left with a neighbor or grandparent while the heavy work is done.

SPECIAL PLACES / NEW HOME

MUSICAL PACKAGES

To make the chore of packing—or unpacking—go faster, try playing this game while the family works together.

- Choose one person to be "it."

- The person who is "it" hums a tune for the others to guess.

- When someone else recognizes the song, he or she shouts "I know the words!" and then proves it by singing back the phrase with the words.

- That person then gets to hum a favorite tune.

A STARRY WELCOME

BEFORE LEAVING YOUR PRESENT HOME

- Spend time as a family outside at night.

- Look at the stars; find the Milky Way, the Big Dipper, the Little Dipper.

- Watch the moon rise, and notice its path and size. Is it full? Quarter?

- Find the North Star, Orion, Cassiopeia.

AFTER ARRIVING AT YOUR NEW HOME

- Leave all the boxes and unpacking for a few minutes each night during the first week.

- Sit quietly as a family in your new yard, on the porch or balcony, or rooftop, if it is safe for everyone.

- Try to find each familiar constellation.

- Talk about the comfort you find in knowing the same sky and heavenly lights are there to welcome you.

- Thank God together for the earth, the sky, and the gift of having each other no matter where you may go.

(If you've moved to another continent, you may find that the summer sky back home is the winter sky of your new home; or the placement of stars may be different.)

NOTE: A whole-family hug is the best warmth on a chilly evening!

SPECIAL PLACES / NEW HOME

GET-ACQUAINTED TREASURE HUNT

- While everyone is busy unloading, hide small surprises or treats around the nooks and crannies of the new house and yard.

- Choose a time when everyone needs a break.

- Give each child a small sack, and send the family out to find the treasures.

- When everyone returns, share the treats and a cool glass of iced tea or lemonade or a cup of hot chocolate, depending on the time of year.

MAKING MEMORIES WITH SPECIAL PEOPLE

GRANDPARENTS / GRANDCHILDREN

FAMILY ROOTS

Most children have very little knowledge of their grandparents' earlier years, yet this background offers one of the richest sources of tradition and identity within a family. Children love to listen to the folklore and the stories that grandparents spin so well, and intergenerational discussions reward everyone with meaningful moments of family history, fun, and love. To give your children this important historical perspective and family bonding:

• Plan a visit to each set of grandparents, prearranging that the theme of the visit will be to have the grandparents share their reminiscences of earlier years and their information about family background.

• Gather the whole family group together after the evening meal (on as many evenings as the length of the visit permits) for a time of listening as the older generation talks. If the visit takes place during cold weather and a fireplace is available, build a fire in the fireplace for the family to gather around.

• A tape recorder or video camera may be used, with the grandparents' permission, to record these priceless memories.

SPECIAL THINGS FOR GRANDPARENTS TO DO WITH GRANDCHILDREN

- Make it a part of every visit to tell your grandchildren (other children, too) some of the things you remember when you were their age that are no longer a part of their lives today. Talk about how things were done, tools and equipment used, various kinds of transportation, family customs and activities, school life, dating and courtship, how you met and married.

- Share a meal each week with your grandchildren (Saturday breakfast, Sunday dinner, Tuesday after-school snack). Make it always the same. Kids love traditions and habits!

- Keep a supply of storybooks. Make it a part of every visit to read a story together with your grandchildren. You do the reading when they're very small. As they learn to read, you can share the reading aloud.

- While they're still small enough to sit on your lap, read the Sunday comics aloud to your grandchildren.

- Let small children name animals while you respond by mimicking the sound that animal makes. Switch roles and let the child make the sounds while you name the animal. Use great drama and animation.

- Take older children (ages 7–15) on bird-watching hikes. Take binoculars and a good bird resource book.

- Take your grandchildren on a nature hike. Take binoculars if you are in an area where wildlife may be seen, and resource books that contain helpful information about what you expect to see. Collect, press, and mount wildflowers in a scrapbook if picking them is allowed in your area.

- Bird, animal, tree, and wildflower resource books may be ordered from the National Wildlife Federation. For information, write to the Federation at: 1412 Sixteenth Street N.W., Washington, D.C. 20036.

GRANDPARENTS / GRANDCHILDREN

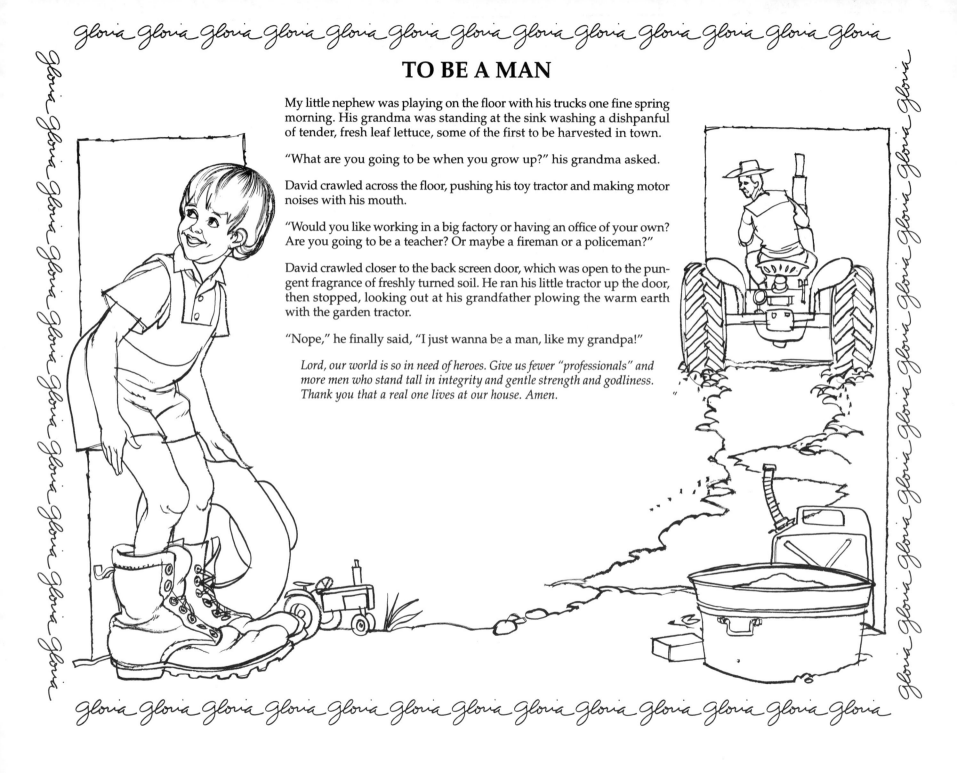

TO BE A MAN

My little nephew was playing on the floor with his trucks one fine spring morning. His grandma was standing at the sink washing a dishpanful of tender, fresh leaf lettuce, some of the first to be harvested in town.

"What are you going to be when you grow up?" his grandma asked.

David crawled across the floor, pushing his toy tractor and making motor noises with his mouth.

"Would you like working in a big factory or having an office of your own? Are you going to be a teacher? Or maybe a fireman or a policeman?"

David crawled closer to the back screen door, which was open to the pungent fragrance of freshly turned soil. He ran his little tractor up the door, then stopped, looking out at his grandfather plowing the warm earth with the garden tractor.

"Nope," he finally said, "I just wanna be a man, like my grandpa!"

Lord, our world is so in need of heroes. Give us fewer "professionals" and more men who stand tall in integrity and gentle strength and godliness. Thank you that a real one lives at our house. Amen.

TREE OF LOVE

MATERIALS NEEDED

Flower pot
Dirt, clay, or plaster of Paris
Small branch
Small slips of paper
Pens
Yarn or ribbon

- Invite a grandparent (or pair of grandparents) for dinner.

- Make a centerpiece that looks like a small tree. This could be a branch anchored in plaster of Paris, or a small plant that resembles a tree; use your imagination.

- Give each family member five slips of paper on which he is asked to write five reasons why his grandparent is special: "I love Grandpa because . . ." or "I love Grandma because . . ."

- Sign each slip, and roll it up like a scroll. Tie it with a colorful ribbon and then attach it to the branches.

- Before dessert, have the grandparent(s) remove and read the slips aloud. Then watch for the sparkle in his or her eyes.

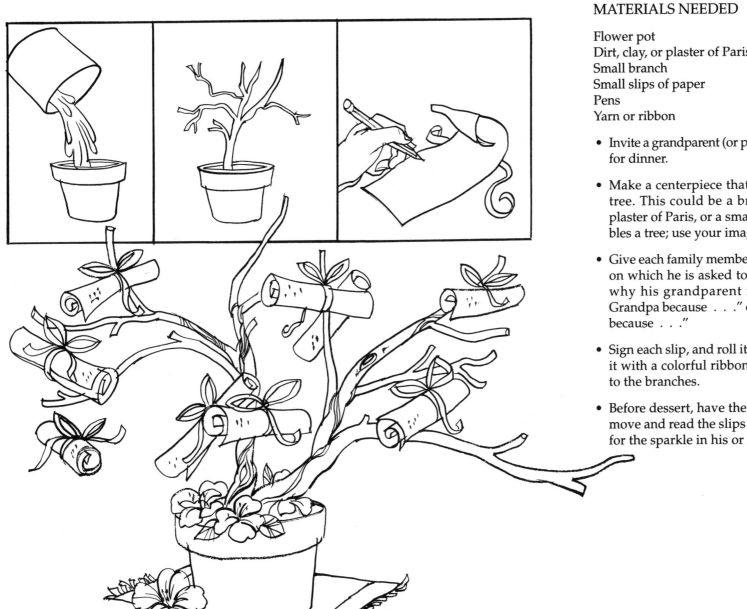

GRANDPARENTS / GRANDCHILDREN

GRANDPARENTS / GRANDCHILDREN

NAMES AND FACES

GRANDPARENTS' NAME CHART

- On a large piece of poster board, draw the first name of a grandparent in big, block letters, 6 or more inches tall, as space permits, arranging the letters vertically or horizontally.

- Inside the letters, draw colorful pictures of the grandparent's favorite foods, clothes, hobbies, sports, or games.

- If you choose to arrange the letters vertically, you may write an acrostic for each letter, naming the many positive qualities of the grandparent.

  EXAMPLE: E elegant, effective, energetic

  L loving, likable, laughing

  S sacrificial, sensible, sweet

  A admirable, attentive, adventuresome

ORIGINAL PORTRAITS

- Have each child draw a picture of the family, including the grandparent(s) in the picture.

- On the bottom of the picture have each child write what the grandparent(s) means to his or her family.

- Mail or give the picture to the grandparent(s).

LOVE LETTERS

As soon as a grandbaby is born, begin to write letters to him or her regularly—every month, every other month, twice a year, etc.

- Tell the child about his or her new abilities or physical development and the joy you feel in watching him or her grow.

- Assure the child of your love.

- Tell the child a little about yourself at this time, and a little about his or her parents.

- Mention the current national events.

NOTE: Parents will want to keep these treasures for the child to enjoy later when he or she is more able to appreciate them. They are good "builder-uppers" when a child is feeling discouraged, ugly, awkward, or afraid of a new situation. This is a good way to keep communications open at every age.

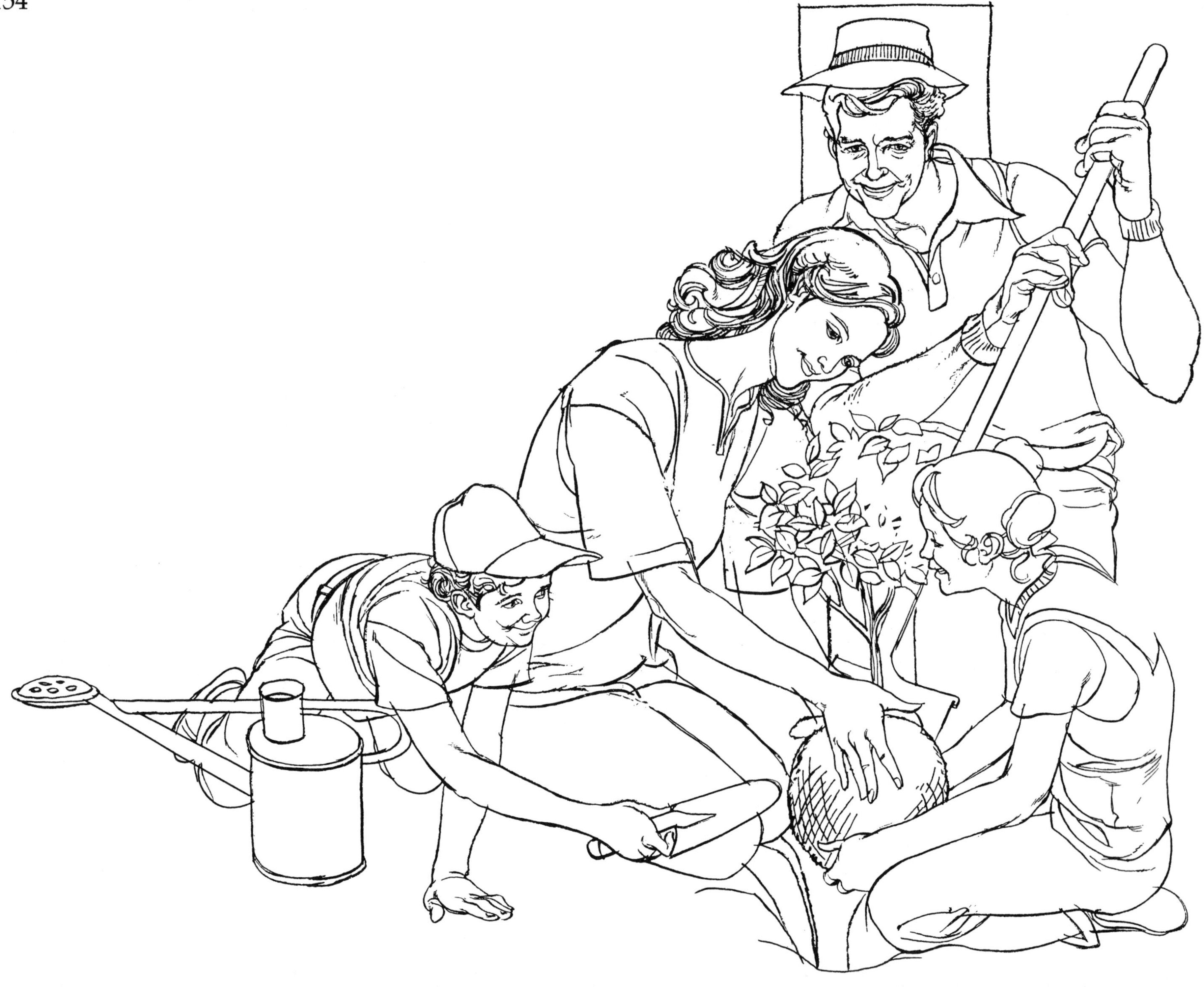

A LIVING WELCOME

In honor of a new baby, make a family project of planting a new tree that will grow as baby grows.

You will need:

> a young tree (this may be a homegrown seedling or a balled-and-burlapped tree from a nursery)
> spades
> small bag of peat moss
> water
> one fertilizer spike formulated for the type of tree you've chosen

- Choose a site for the tree that will allow plenty of room for growth and spreading. Be realistic; notice the size of full-grown trees of this species, or ask your nurseryman for information.

- Dig a hole approximately $1\frac{1}{2}$ times as wide and as deep as the balled roots or twice as large as the root system of a seedling. Take turns digging, letting younger children help too.

- Sprinkle a good layer of peat moss in the bottom of the hole.

- Set the tree into the hole, letting the bottom of the roots touch the peat moss. If the roots are not balled, be sure to gently spread them, taking care to see that they are not broken or crowded.

- Check to see that the crown of the root system or the top of the balled roots is just slightly lower than the top surface of the ground.

- Fill the hole half full of water.

- Sprinkle loose soil into the hole until the hole is filled. As you fill, form a sort of saucer around the tree trunk that will hold water.

- Carefully water the tree again, filling the saucer but not so full that it runs over. As the water seeps in, it will naturally pack the soil around the roots so you will not need to press the soil down and run the danger of breaking the tender roots. After the water has seeped in, you may need to add a little more soil, but be sure to maintain the saucer.

- Insert one fertilizer spike just inside the rim of the soil saucer.

- Water each day by filling the saucer with water until the tree has a good start, then water whenever the weather is dry.

When the baby grows old enough to understand, tell him or her about the tree and that it was planted by those who love him or her most. Thank God for the joy of working with Him in the creation and nurturing process. Thank Him together for the new life that has come to be a part of your family. Promise to nurture each other through the "seasons" of your lives.

VARIATION

Make a tradition of planting a tree for each child in the family when he or she reaches age six (or whatever age you desire).

You may want to plant the same variety of tree each time—all pines, all hardwoods, fruit trees for an orchard, etc. Give the child in whose honor the tree is planted the responsibility of keeping it watered until it has a good start.

- Take a picture of the tree as it is being planted and keep it in a scrapbook.

- Take pictures periodically of the tree's growth.

- After the tree begins to mature, take pictures of it at different seasons.

- When the child is older, invite him or her to write about the tree. Add this writing to the scrapbook as well.

FAMILY

FAMILY

NEW BABY WELCOME BANNER

To welcome a new baby to the world, make a baby banner. This is a great activity for fathers to do with the other children in the family while Mom is at the hospital with the new baby. It is also a good project for the family to do together while waiting for a baby who is to be adopted.

- Obtain a large sheet of poster board or sheet of banquet table paper.

- Spread a protective layer of newspapers on the floor or the driveway.

- Let the children create a design and choose a slogan.

- Pencil it onto the banner.

- Use markers or tempera paints to create a colorful message. Have fun, and share the clean-up.

- Hang the banner over the crib in the baby's room.

- You can also print a banner using computer graphics software, then have fun coloring or painting it in party colors.

SUGGESTIONS FOR BANNER SLOGANS

Welcome to the Fortner Family!
You're with Us, Baby!
You Can Voice Your Opinion Here!
It's Time for Timothy!
Building Site: Tommy Growing Here!
Sherri Is Something Special!
Patty's a Promise!

DAD'S TREAT

Here are some special things for fathers to do with kids:

- Pack a "Dad's Day" picnic and go to a surprise place to eat it:

  a park
  an empty lot
  the woods
  a lake

- Take your son or daughter for a "dad-type" shopping trip to find one special item:

  a doll
  a new part for an electric train
  a model to build
  drumsticks or guitar strings
  a new dress
  tennis shoes
  first basketball or first baseball mitt

  Have lunch together afterward at a fancy place or favorite hamburger shop.

- Plan a "dads' special outing" with another father and son or daughter:

  go to a ball game
  go to a car race
  go to a wrestling match
  take a nature hike
  go mountain climbing
  take a fishing trip

- Rent a movie or video tape from the library or from a rental store. Dads might enjoy sharing with the family:

  nature films
  live concerts by family favorites
  music groups
  old home movies taken when parents or
      kids were younger

- Make it Dad's task to wake up the kids every morning by rubbing their backs or singing a silly wake-up song, or by raising the blinds and saying, "This is the day the Lord hath made!"

FAMILY

FAMILY

APPRECIATION TIME

HELPING HANDS

- Trace Mother's, Dad's, or grandparents' hands on a folded piece of 8 ½" x 11" paper. Draw one hand on the front of the paper and one on the back; the inside of the folded paper will be used for a message (see below).

- Let the child color the hand picture, drawing in the parent's watch, ring, fingernails, etc.

- Help the child compose a note to put inside the paper that shows appreciation for the loving things that are done by the person whose hands have been traced: fixing dinner, ironing, putting on Band-Aids, making repairs on the house, fixing toys, reading stories, etc.

- At the bottom of the page, write, "We appreciate you, Mom (Dad, Grandpa, etc.)!"

- Give as a special-occasion card.

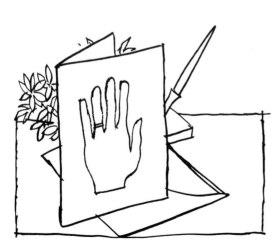

FAMILY CARD FOR MOTHER'S DAY / FATHER'S DAY

- Fold a large sheet (12" x 18") of construction paper in half.

- Decorate the front of the card with a greeting or picture. If the parent has a hobby, perhaps a picture related to that activity would be appropriate.

- Glue a snapshot of each person in the family inside the card and have each person write a message of love under his or her picture. These messages might all begin "You're special to me because . . ." or "One reason I love you so is . . ." or "I remember when you . . ."

THANK YOU FOR "ME"

It's fun for a child to receive gifts on his or her birthday, but it will be even more meaningful to Mother to receive something special from the child whose birthday it is.

- On *your* birthday, send a corsage, bouquet of flowers, card, or other remembrance to your mother.

- Include a note saying, "Thank you for giving birth to me."

PROMISE COUPONS

For Father's Day or Mother's Day, make a coupon book filled with some promises to give the gift of yourself in time and energy to do helpful things. These coupons may be used any time in the next year.

- Cut blank index cards into equal coupon-size pieces.

- On each card write "This coupon good for . . . ," naming one chore or favor:

  doing dinner dishes one time
  cleaning the garage
  raking leaves for one hour
  one car wash
  one hour of window washing
  one hour of playing Scrabble (or other game of your choice)
  one week of feeding the dog

- Save one coupon piece to make an attractive cover for the coupon book.

- Staple all the coupons together and put the coupon book in an envelope.

- Tie a ribbon around the envelope and lay it on the parent's plate before dinner or breakfast of the special day.

SEVENTEEN

The first day of school didn't start until one o'clock, so there was plenty of time for breakfast at McDonald's and shopping for the supplies that had been listed in the *Times-Tribune* the Wednesday before. You reminded us to go to McDonald's for breakfast. "We've always gone there on the first day of school," you said. Something hard to label stirred inside me when you said it. Perhaps it was pride—pride that you still found joy in our crazy little tradition; or perhaps it was pleasure—pleasure in knowing that you still choose to be with our family when you have your "druthers." But there was a certain sadness, too, and I couldn't stop the knowing this was your last first day of school.

You came down the stairs that morning all neat and well-groomed, the healthy glow of your summer tan and freckles still showing through your make-up, your sun-bleached hair carefully arranged. "Hi, Mom" you said, and your grin showed your straight, white teeth. No more orthodontist appointments, I thought, and no more broken glasses to glue before school. Contacts and braces had sure been worth it.

"I've got to have my senior pictures taken tomorrow after school, Mom. Can I use the car?" "As far as I know," I answered, then reminded you of your promise to take your sister to get her hair trimmed at three o'clock that afternoon. Your driver's license had come in handy, too.

By then Amy and Benjy were ready, and we all piled into the car and drove to McDonald's. As we ate, we talked about other first days—the first day of kindergarten, the first day of junior high, and that scary first day in the big new high school. You all interrupted each other with stories of embarrassing moments, awards, friendships, and fright.

After we had eaten, we hurried to buy notebook paper and compasses before I dropped you all at school—first Amy and Benjy at the middle school, then you. "'Bye, Mom," you said as you scooted across the seat. Then you stopped a moment and looked back over your shoulder. "And, Mom . . . thanks." It was the remnant of a kiss good-bye. It was the hesitancy of a little girl in ringlets beginning kindergarten. It was the anticipation of a young woman confident of her direction—these were all there in that gesture.

"I love you," was all I answered, but I had hoped that somehow you could hear with your heart the rest of the words that were going through my mind—words that told you how special you are to us; words that would let you know how rich your father and I have been because you came into our lives; words that tell you how much we believe in you, hope for you, pray for you, thank God for you. As the school doors closed behind you and you disappeared into the corridor, I wanted so to holler after you: "*Wait!* We have so much yet to do. We've never been to Hawaii. We've never taken a cruise. That book of poetry we wrote together isn't published yet. And what about the day we were going to spend at the cabin just being still and reading? Or the writers' workshop we planned to attend together in Illinois? You can't go yet . . . WAIT!"

But I knew you couldn't wait, and that we could never keep you by calling a halt to your progress. You had promises to keep.

The things we want to save, Jesus has said, must be let go of, for the things we hold most tightly will be strangled in the end. And so, though I knew this was a last first, I also somehow knew that it was a first in a whole lifetime of new beginnings . . . and I rejoiced!

YOU ARE SPECIAL

Children are special, and this is an extra special way to show them that they are.

- Tell the children *special* people are coming to dinner, people you love more than anyone in the world.

- Have the children bathe, put on their nicest dress clothes, and hide in their rooms "until the company comes."

- While preparing their favorite meal, set the table with your best linens, china, crystal, candles, and fresh flowers.

- Make crowns as place cards and print their names on them: "King Robert" or "Queen Kimberly."

- When the meal is ready, call them and tell them the company is here. When they run out and ask, "Where are they?", tell them, "*You* are the guests of honor." Treat them like royalty that evening. This is a beautiful way to say "I love you."

FAMILY

FAMILY

MY SPECIAL DINNER

- Once a month, have each child prepare the evening menu for the family. (If there are two children in the family, this will involve two evenings a month; if there are three children, three evenings will be required, and so on.)

- Let the child help you shop for the groceries and help prepare the food and design special table decorations.

- Suggest that it will be fun to keep the menu a secret from the rest of the family until dinnertime.

- Use this project as a means for the child to learn about nutrition, about the effort necessary to prepare meals, the expense of food, methods of attractive preparation, etc.

THE V.I.P.

- Choose a smooth block of wood, a beautiful rock, a slice of a small log, etc.

- Using wood-burning tools, enamel paint, or markers, write a V.I.P. message for Dad's or Mom's desk, kitchen window, motor home, or van.

- Grandparents, aunts, and uncles will be proud to have one of these too.

FAMILY

SECOND HONEYMOON

There is nothing better for kids than parents who love each other! Help parents stay in love by encouraging them to take a second honeymoon. Finding out where your parents went on their first honeymoon and whether they would enjoy going back to the same place might help you with your "promotion."

- Collect travel folders from the travel bureau.

- Volunteer to take extra responsibility for taking care of things while they are gone.

- Volunteer to give up something so they can use the money to go or plan a special project such as a garage sale to help make money.

- Go together with your brothers and sisters to buy Mom a new nightgown or some perfume and Dad some cologne or a new swimsuit.

TO MOM FROM TAMMY AND ERIN

KEEPING ROMANCE ALIVE

MONTHLY ANNIVERSARY

Here is a simple tradition that can help renew and keep alive your romantic relationship. Every month, on the day numbered the same as your wedding day, repeat a simple pattern; for instance, on the tenth of each month:

- Bring home a rose.

- Put a love note in the lunch pail.

- Go out for the evening, or promise a night out at a mutually agreed-upon time.

- Just whisper a question, worded the same way every month, such as "Do you know what day this is?"

A ROMANTIC TRAVEL TOUCH

- When going on an overnight trip or vacation, tuck a candle and an attractive candleholder into your luggage.

- At bedtime, light the candle and enjoy the restful and soothing atmosphere. Candlelight adds a romantic touch to the surroundings whether you are in a motel or a camper.

- Make this a way of telling your spouse that he or she is loved and still romantically attractive to you.

"OUR SONG"

- Select a special love song that has meaning to both of you.

- Buy a record of that song or, if you have a piano or other instrument, learn to play it yourself.

- Hearing that song played and sung can often give your love an identity and help you through the ups and downs of everyday living.

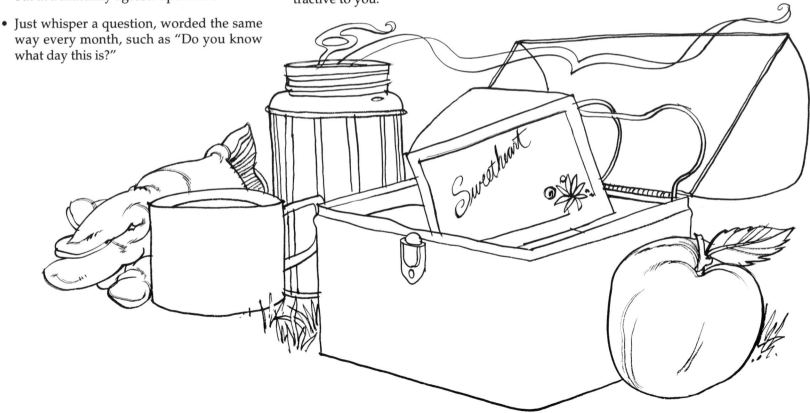

HUSBANDS AND WIVES

KEEPING ROMANCE ALIVE (cont.)

THOUGHTFUL IDEAS FOR DAD

- A simple "thank you" kiss for Mom from Dad after a meal not only expresses gratitude to Mom, but it tells the kids that their parents love each other and appreciate each other.

- On your way home from work, pick up some bath crystals for your wife. Volunteer to care for the children while she leisurely enjoys her gift.

- If you have a new baby in your family, before your wife and new baby arrive home from the hospital, write a love note and leave it on the bedroom pillow. Welcome them home and pledge your love and care. The new mother will feel valued and will be pleasantly surprised. Then, tuck the message away in a keepsake file.

A TIME FOR JUST YOU AND ME

When Jim and I were first married, he was finishing his graduate training and I was busily teaching school. These career objectives forced us to postpone the experience of parenthood for a few years. We were extremely busy, but we were able to steal away for an occasional carefree weekend together. We would wander through department stores, holding hands, laughing, and talking. We loved to window-shop for furniture and dream about how we hoped to decorate our house of the future. We would enjoy a light breakfast and then plan a candlelit dinner somewhere for the evening.

Many years have passed now—and such relaxing times are even more difficult to achieve. Although our children are grown now and live away from home, there are still the pressures of Jim's work. God has blessed our ministry far more than we ever dreamed possible, but the demands are many. We take several trips during a typical year but usually with obligations to be faced upon arrival. I must admit there are times when I *long* for just the two of us to get away again and spend a relaxed, self-indulgent weekend together. I remember one special time when we were able to do just that.

Mammoth ski resort was a six-hour drive from our house in California. After arranging for my mother to care for the children, we loaded the car and headed for our winter wonderland. I felt like a college girl again. We talked along the way and stopped to eat whenever it suited our fancy.

The next morning, we donned our colorful ski clothes and headed for our favorite restaurant, The Swiss Café. Hilda, the bubbly Swedish lady who owned the restaurant, called me "Shoooolie." During our visits there we had come to love her.

Our conversation at the breakfast table took us into each other's worlds, again. Jim's eyes never looked bluer, and the love that's always there between us, steady and committed, surged to an emotional peak.

Driving to the ski lodge was equally exhilarating. The roads looked like a Currier and Ives Christmas card. The giant evergreens appeared majestic in their white fur coats. I knew it was going to be a great day for skiing. The sky was blue and the snow was a skier's paradise. Once on the mountain, we swished back and forth across the mountain like two adolescents. The snow was so "forgiving" we could do nothing wrong.

We were wonderfully exhausted driving back to the condo. Jim prepared a cozy fire in the fireplace while I made our favorite meal of fried burritos. We set up a card table and ate dinner by the firelight, discussing the good and bad skiing techniques of our day and an endless variety of other topics.

After the dinner dishes were cleaned up, we pulled the pillows off the couch, chose some of our favorite records and put them on the stereo. While relaxing by the fire, we promised each other we would try to repeat this private rendezvous at least once a year.

Believe me, the memories of that weekend motivated me for days afterward to be the wife and mother I needed to be.

As important as traditions are in a family, husbands and wives need romantic involvement when they are alone—a time when the children are not even thought of. This is good therapy not only for busy adults, but for their kids as well.

NEIGHBORS

FLOWER FESTIVAL

- Buy flowering bedding plants—marigolds, petunias, geraniums, or other favorites—or start your own from seed.

- Go as a family to someone you love, then work together to fill his or her outside planters or window boxes.

  NOTE: If your friend has no containers, this annual activity could begin with the gift of a container.

- Follow these steps:

  1. Fill the container with soil and mix in suitable fertilizer.

  2. Carefully separate the plants and arrange them in the container, giving attention to expected height and color of the plants.

  3. Water carefully.

  4. Clean up any spilled soil, and carry away empty plant cartons.

- After the planting is done, share some lemonade.

BLOCK PARTY

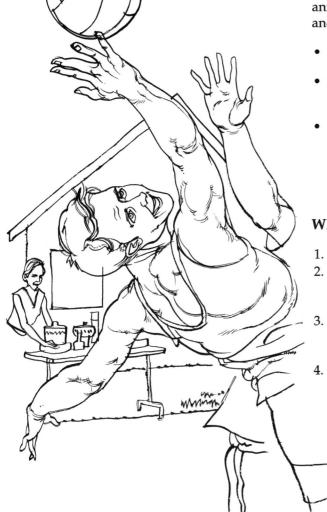

A block party is a great way for neighbors to get acquainted, and one that creates a good neighborhood feeling. You can organize a simple get-together on your own for a starter. After the ice is broken, the whole group of neighbors will probably want to share in making a block party an annual affair, with a committee to choose a place, a date, and a time, and to coordinate a menu and other responsibilities. For a simple block party:

- Invite each family on the block to come to your house, bringing their own favorite dessert.

- Provide stick-on name tags (unless your neighborhood has been so stable that everyone knows each other).

- Arrange for a get-acquainted mixer (if neighbors are not well known to each other) or other fun group activity such as charades or a fast game of volleyball. You might want to try the popular icebreaker described below, which is sure to get everyone acquainted. The object is to have all of the guests introduce themselves to each other and to learn a little about each person.

WHAT'S MY NAME ICEBREAKER

1. Draw a chart of 1" to 2" squares on a sheet of paper. Make at least one square per guest.
2. At the top of each square write in a characteristic that could possibly fit one of your guests. (See suggestions below.) These can be designed to be humorous, or, if practical, the chart can be prepared to provide an interesting fact about each guest, making sure no one is omitted.
3. When guests arrive, provide each one with a pencil and a copy of the chart. Explain that they are to circulate among the group, meeting as many people as possible and asking questions that will help them fill in the blanks on the chart.
4. When the allotted time is up, find out who has the most squares filled in and ask him or her to read aloud the name and corresponding statement in each of the squares. Have each person stand as his or her name is called. If not all the guests have been introduced in this way, have the remaining ones stand and introduce themselves individually.

Talks back to TV commercials	Can wiggle ears	Can touch palms to floor
Has a hole in the bottom of his shoe now	Hates hamburgers	Runs 15 miles or more a day

NEIGHBORS

NEIGHBORS

TRAVELING FRIENDSHIP BASKET

Starting a Traveling Friendship Basket on its way through your neighborhood offers a good way to "reach out and touch" each other in friendship.

- Buy a large, inexpensive basket.

- Tie a cheerfully colored ribbon on it, along with directions asking the recipient to send it on to its next destination.

- The family starting the basket prepares the contents with their next-door neighbors in mind. For example: if the basket will be going to a family with children, fill it with brownies; if the basket is to go to a widow, fill it with a beautiful bouquet from your flower garden; if you sew, send it along with a practical creation for the home.

- The recipients are then asked to pass the basket to the neighbors on the other side of them (not the neighbors from whom they received the basket), again trying to fill it with contents appropriate for that neighbor or items that represent the special talents of the new donors.

- Keep the basket moving. Try not to let more than a week go by before sending it on.

- When the basket reaches the end of the block, send it to the family across the street and move it in the opposite direction so that it travels in a continuous circuit. The distance it travels can be greater than one block, of course, but it may be helpful to establish some kind of limit.

ESPECIALLY FOR FAMILIES TO DO WITH AN OLDER NEIGHBOR

Many older people have lost a spouse or close friends and also have more difficulty getting out than they did when they were younger. This can be a lonely time. Include them in some of your activities! Here are some ways:

- Invite your friend to go along with your family to the Dairy Queen, or drop by with an ice cream cone if he or she can't get out.

- Drop by now and then when you or your family are out riding bikes.

- Invite your friend to your birthday party. Make sure he or she has a hat to wear and a horn to blow like everyone else.

- Volunteer to mow the grass, clip around lamp posts, pull some weeds, or paint the mailbox.

- Mail unexpected notes or cards—valentines, Easter cards, school pictures, etc.

- Share a tape recording (provide a cassette player if needed) of a concert, church service, school program, band recital, etc.

- Ask your friend's opinion of a paper, a poem, or song you've written.

- Drop by with one or two of your friends so that your friend can meet them. Make your visits short.

- Offer to pick the cherries, sweep the driveway, wash the car, clean the windows on the outside, shake the rugs, run an errand.

Some of your neighbors, especially elderly ones, may have weak or blind eyes. Offer to provide "eyes" for them by volunteering to do the following things:

- Have a "read-in" once or twice a week. Suggest to the friend for whom you are reading that he or she invite other friends to share in the "read-in." Choose a "book-of-the-month" that all will enjoy having read aloud.

- Volunteer to write and mail letters or to help with the correspondence involved in paying bills.

- Give a subscription to a large-print edition of a good magazine such as *Reader's Digest* or *Guideposts*. Order from:

  Reader's Digest Fund for the Blind
  Large-Type Publication
  P.O. Box 241
  Mt. Morris, IL 61054

  Guideposts
  Big Print Edition
  Carmel, NY 10512

NEIGHBORS

NEIGHBORS

GOOD FEELINGS

Helpers like the mailman, gardener, policeman, fireman, and others contribute much to the well-being of the neighborhood. Show appreciation and encourage good feelings.

- On a hot summer day, prepare a cool glass of punch or lemonade to give to the letter carrier when he or she comes, to the gardener who is working outside, to the police officer who walks the beat in your neighborhood, etc.

- A neighbor who is doing outdoor chores on a hot day will also appreciate a refreshing cold drink or even a brief helping hand. A moment of thoughtfulness builds good feelings among neighbors.

UNUSUAL WAYS TO SAY "GET WELL"

LEAVES OF LOVE

- On poster board, draw a large tree with bare limbs only.

- Cut out 10 to 20 leaves from green or multi-colored construction paper. Make them large enough to write on.

- Have each family member write a love note, joke, or riddle on a leaf. Repeat until all the much appreciated leaves are used. Pin the leaves on the branches.

- Hang the tree in the patient's room. Be sure to place it where he or she can read it easily.

SNAPSHOT OF CHEER

Instead of taking or sending candy or flowers to a loved one or neighbor who is in the hospital, stop by the patient's home with your camera and take several pictures of his or her family. Have the film developed and printed and give the pictures to the patient. He or she will love showing them to the nurses and other friends, who drop by, and your thoughtfulness will be much appreciated.

LEAVES OF LOVE

PEOPLE WHO ARE ILL

HOMEY COMFORTS FOR A SICK CHILD

Sick days—and nights—are no fun. Help them pass faster for your child.

- Read aloud the child's favorite books.

- To soothe a fever, dampen a washcloth with cold water, squeeze it out thoroughly, and place it on the patient's forehead.

- Sleep in the room with the child when there is a possibility of his or her vomiting, which can be a frightening experience for a child.

- When the child's stomach has settled, a small amount of scraped apple may be offered.

  Cut top edge from the apple.
  With spoon tip, scrape the apple meat from inside the peel and feed it to the child.

- Make hot "milk-toast" and spoon-feed to the patient.

  Place one slice of buttered toast in a shallow bowl. Pour steaming hot (but not boiled) milk over toast. When it's cool enough to eat, offer small bites to the patient with a spoon.

LAP TABLE

It is sometimes difficult to keep an active child as quiet as he or she needs to be during a minor illness or recuperation from something more serious. A lap table is a big help.

- Make a lap table from a cardboard box with arches cut out of it to enable the box to fit over a child's legs.

- Spray paint the table with a bright color and allow it to dry thoroughly.

- Turn the lap table upside down. There should be ample room to place a smaller box (a shoebox is a good size) inside the lap table to be used as a sick-day busy box.

- Fill the box with suitable craft materials:

    newspapers (to protect the bed)
    scissors
    paste or Elmer's glue
    bits of yarn
    buttons
    crayons or felt markers
    small pieces of cloth
    construction paper
    magazines with lots of pictures (for
        cutting up)
    small package of tissue

- Use the box and lap table for craft activities only. Keep it put away until needed.

- When the lap table is needed, remove the inside box and place it within easy reach of the child. Place the lap table over his or her lap.

- Suggest things for the child to make—collages, puzzles, scrapbooks, drawings, etc. He or she will stay quietly busy for hours.

SUGGESTION: Lap tables make a great family gift for anyone who is ill. The shoebox insert can be filled with "grown-up" articles such as lip balm, body lotions, powder, tissues, comb, mirror, etc., as well as craft items or writing materials desired by the patient.

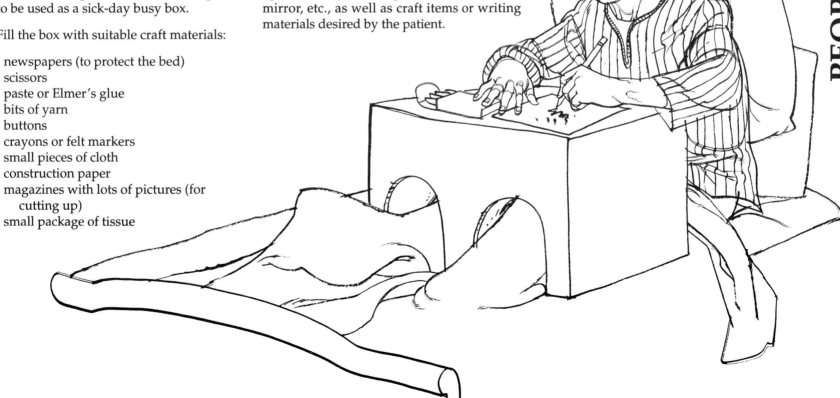

IDEAS FOR CHILDREN WITH A
PROLONGED ILLNESS

- Send a small gift each day through the mail—a piece of gum, bookmark, balloon, package of plant seeds, miniature puzzle, lollipop, etc.

- Fill a variety box with the materials for making drawings, collages, posters, and constructing small objects: scissors, crayons, paper, pins, material, buttons, needles, thread, magnifying glass, mirror, pieces of aluminum foil, flashlight, box of paper clips, clay, paper hole-punch, toothpicks, glue, gummed stars, stickers, etc.

- Plant a garden indoors. Place two or three pieces of dampened cotton in a glass. Push a grapefruit seed, a pea, or a bean into the cotton. Keep cotton moist and watch the sprout grow!

JUST WHAT THE DOCTOR ORDERED

- Cut narrow strips of colored paper about four inches long.

- Write or type on each paper some personal word of encouragement, a Bible verse, or some other quotation.

- Roll up each strip of paper as tightly as possible, drop a tiny spot of rubber cement on the end and wrap it with a twist-tie (from a box of plastic bags). Remove the twist ties when the rubber cement dries.

- Fill a small box with the "medicinal" scrolls and give it to the patient with instructions to "take one every four hours, three times a day," or on a schedule that will fit the probable length of the patient's stay in bed.

EXAMPLE: "You're the best sister a guy could have. I love you."

"When you get well, I promise to treat you to an ice cream cone at Barkley's."

"Thanks for all the times you've helped me with my math. I'm glad you're so smart!"

"My heart shall rejoice in thy salvation" (Ps. 13:5).

"I will sing unto the Lord for He hath dealt bountifully with me" (Ps. 13:6).

"The Lord is my light and my salvation; whom shall I fear? The Lord is the strength of my life; of whom shall I be afraid?" (Ps. 27:1).

PEOPLE WHO ARE ILL

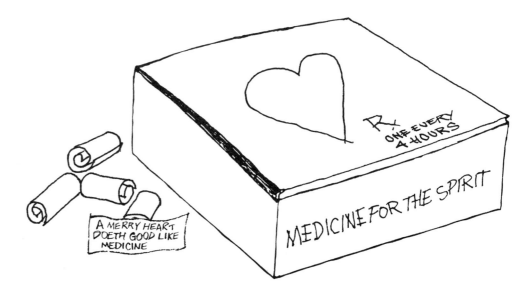

WHEN YOU'RE FEELING BETTER

BAKED PLAY DOUGH COOKIES

- Give the child a cookie sheet, homemade play dough (recipe below), and a few cookie cutters.

- Cut out play dough cookies and place on the baking sheet. Bake.

- Cool and decorate the cookies with poster paint or marker pens.

PLAY DOUGH RECIPE

4 cups flour
1 cup salt
1½ cups water (add more if needed)
(For colored dough, add a few drops of food coloring to the water.)

After the dough is molded or cut into the desired shapes, bake at 325 degrees for 2 to 3 hours until it is hardened.

NOTE: This mixture is *not* to be eaten, but is intended for crafts only.

PITCH A PENNY

- Place a large can on the floor near the sick child's bed.

- Give the child a handful of pennies.

- Have the child see how many pennies he or she can pitch into the can.

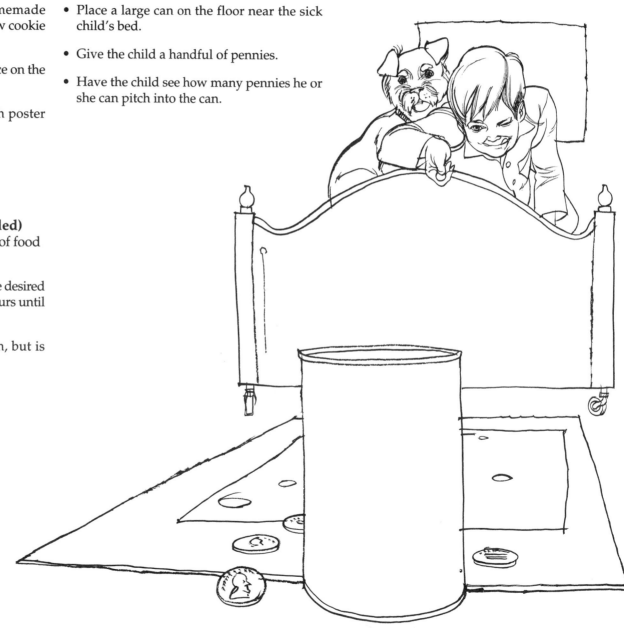

MAKING MEMORIES IN GOD'S WORD

"JESUS IS LIGHT"

- Place a candle on the table for a centerpiece. Let the candle provide the *only* light for the meal.

- Have one family member read aloud Isaiah 9:2–7. Talk about how the world was in darkness before He came. Jesus brought light; Jesus *is* light.

- Discuss the fact that most people in the world even today have less light than we do. Many have no electricity but use candles or oil lamps.

- Point out also that most of the world has not heard the gospel, as we have in this country.

- Pray a special prayer about light. Use this one or one of your own:

Thank You for the light of the gospel. Help us send it to the world's dark places as well as to those who live in darkness all around us.

OBJECT LESSON IN GOD'S WORD

- Prepare an obstacle course in a hallway, using toys, chairs, books, and boxes placed in such a way as to make it difficult to get through.

- Turn off all the lights.

- In turn, let each family member walk or crawl through the hallway.

- Next, let someone lead the way with a flashlight.

- Turn on the lights. Discuss how it felt to get through the maze in the dark. Was it difficult? How did you feel when the flashlight was used?

- In the Bible, turn to Psalm 119:105 and John 8:12. Read the verses aloud.

- Discuss how God's Word can lead us through the "dark places" in life; how it "lights" our path and gives us direction.

GOD'S WORD / LIGHT

TWENTY QUESTIONS

Play this familiar game choosing a biblical character or object as the secret to be guessed.

- Draw straws to determine who will be "it," the person who chooses the secret.

- Have the other members of the family guess who or what the secret is by asking twenty questions that can be answered by a simple yes or no.

- Each family member asks one question in turn.

- Whoever guesses correctly before the twentieth question becomes "it," and gets the next turn to choose a secret.

- If no one guesses the secret in twenty questions, the person who is "it" is the winner, and he or she chooses another person to be "it."

LEARNING GOD'S WORD TOGETHER

- Choose a Bible verse to memorize.

- Have someone in the family circle say the first word of the verse.

- Continue around the circle with each person saying the next word until the verse has been completed.

- Each time the verse is rehearsed, start with a different family member until each person has learned the verse.

- This is also a fun way to learn the names of the books of the Bible.

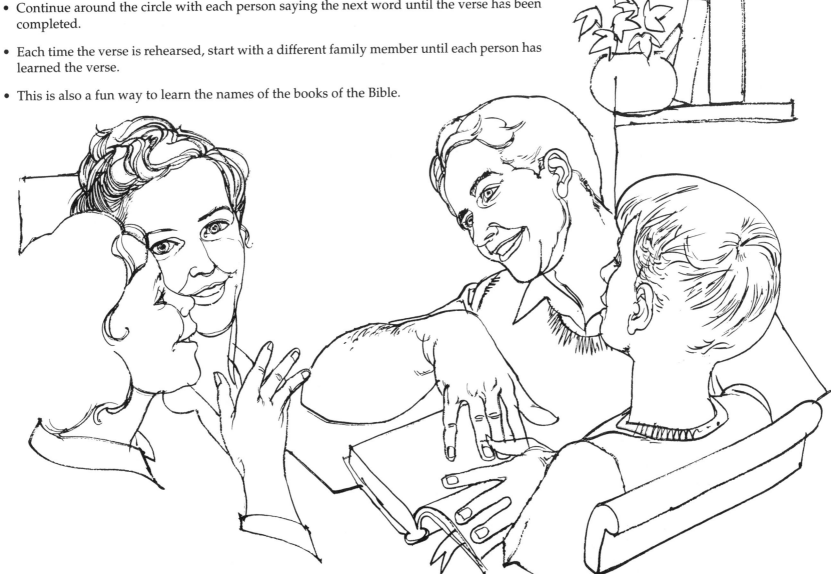

GOD'S WORD / MEMORY LEARNING

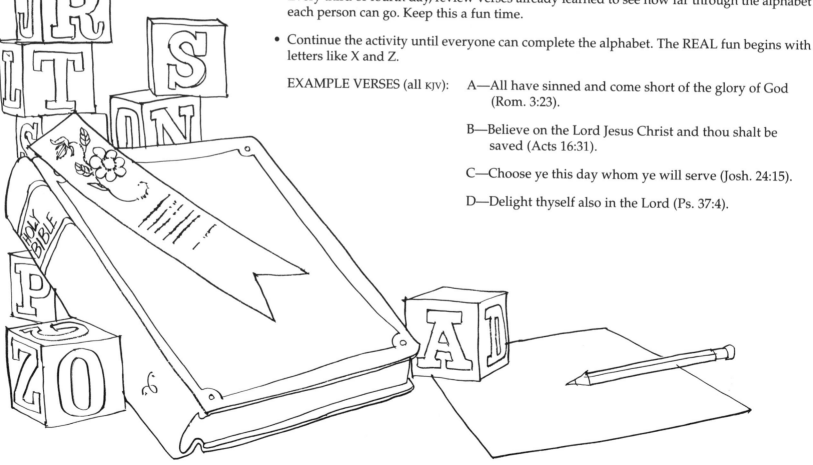

GOD'S WORD / MEMORY LEARNING

THE BIBLE ALPHABET

- To do this activity, choose a special day of the week that will suit your family.

- Have each member of the family choose and memorize a Bible verse that begins with the letter *A*. The verse that is chosen must be a complete sentence.

- At a certain time of day (breakfast, supper, bedtime, or whatever time the family chooses) have each person recite his or her verse.

- The next week, learn verses beginning with *B*, and the following week learn verses beginning with *C*, and so on.

- Every third or fourth day, review verses already learned to see how far through the alphabet each person can go. Keep this a fun time.

- Continue the activity until everyone can complete the alphabet. The REAL fun begins with letters like X and Z.

EXAMPLE VERSES (all KJV): A—All have sinned and come short of the glory of God (Rom. 3:23).

B—Believe on the Lord Jesus Christ and thou shalt be saved (Acts 16:31).

C—Choose ye this day whom ye will serve (Josh. 24:15).

D—Delight thyself also in the Lord (Ps. 37:4).

WORD CUP

The object of this game is to recall a Bible verse based on a key word that is contained in the verse or that pertains to the thought of the verse. This game is ideal for mealtime or anytime the family is gathered together.

- Print "key" words on slips of paper or tiny squares of poster board. (The cardboard that backs memo pads or legal pads will work.)

- Put the words in a teacup or mug.

- Pass the cup around the dinner table asking each person (guests, too) to take one word.

- At the end of dinner, ask each person to take a turn recalling a verse from the Bible (or an incident) that contains that word or speaks to that subject.

- Some words that might be used are:

    heart
    sin
    body
    liars
    worry
    children

- Suggested subjects could be:

    honesty
    obedience
    time management
    friends
    forgiveness

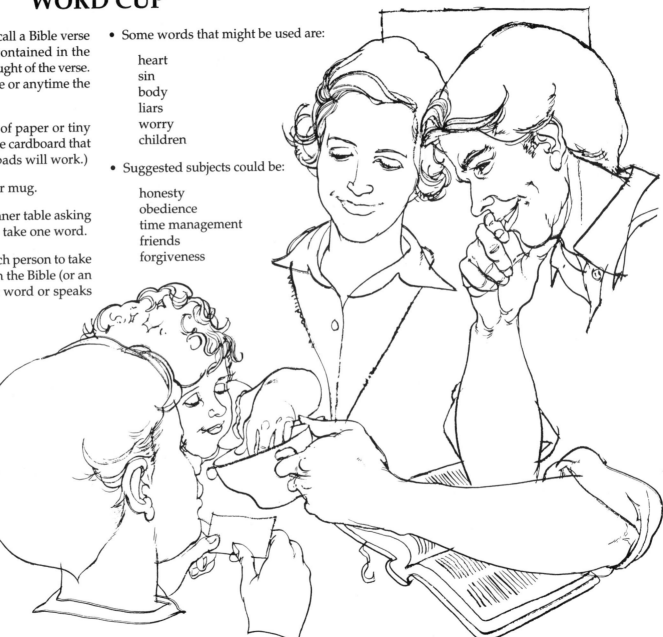

GOD'S WORD / MEMORY LEARNING

MYSTERY VERSE

- Choose a Bible verse.

- Write each word of the verse on a separate card.

- Spread the cards on the table in correct order.

- Remove three or four cards.

- See who can say the whole verse filling in the "mystery" words from memory.

KEEPING MEMORIES ALIVE

TIME TO REMINISCE

- Before grown children arrive for a visit, get out things you made together or collected as they were growing up. Have these things displayed in a special room (den, living room, screened front porch, etc.). Some things might be:

    baby books and scrapbooks
    sports or achievement awards, report cards, medals, graduation dresses, first baseball
        uniforms, first ice skates, etc.
    birthday flags (see page 67)
    New Year's diaries (see page 18)
    summer memory books (see page 98)
    vacation diaries (see page 125)
    soil diaries (see page 127)
    memory collages (see page 124)
    prize prints (see page 137)

- Fill a big wicker basket full of popcorn and spend some happy hours remembering and celebrating the gift of being a family.

    BONUS: If there are grandchildren, this is a special time for them to get to know something about what their parents were like as children and what they did then.

FAMILY REUNION

Make this a very special occasion by sharing not only food but the reliving and creation of memories.

- Share a meal, each bringing his or her best dish.

- Have a short devotion including singing accompanied by piano, guitar, and/or other instruments played by family members.

- Go around the family circle, each person telling the most important thing that has happened in his or her life since all were last together.

- Have a "talent show" with at least one contribution from each grown child and/or the new family he or she represents and from each parent.

MEMORIES / KEEP ALIVE

THE FAMILY THAT PLAYS TOGETHER . . .

Play is just as important for adults in building and maintaining healthy relationships as it is for children. When the family clan is together, make time for play. Try any or all of the following:

- Table games such as Roll-a-Role, Scrabble, Strategy, Rook, Monopoly, Trivial Pursuit, Pictionary, Jenga.

- Puzzles (large, time-consuming jigsaw puzzles offer a wonderful opportunity for conversation).

- Outside games such as kickball, softball, volleyball, tennis, badminton, etc.

- Fishing and camping (even backyard camping).

- Sidewalk art contests. (Give everyone a dime store box of colored chalk with which to create a driveway or sidewalk "masterpiece." Have a neighbor judge the prettiest, funniest, most unique. The first rainstorm will erase the art, but for a few days you can enjoy the sidewalk gallery.)

- Ditch-um. (This is a team version of hide-and-go seek played at night from a "home base." Since the "seekers" are a team, young children can team up with the grownups and feel safe.)

- Roller skating party (on the sidewalks in your neighborhood, on a large driveway, at an empty parking lot, or at a roller rink).

- Sledding party (with hot chocolate and a warming bonfire where fires are allowed).

- Clambake (see page 135).

SHARE A PROJECT

Save a special project to be done when grown children (and perhaps *their* children) come home. Here are some suggestions:

- Cut, saw, and split a tree for the winter's supply of firewood. This is a great time to teach youngsters how to prepare firewood and at the same time share physical labor. A grown son or daughter and his or her father or mother could find this a good time for conversation, too.

- Plant something together: a tree, berry bushes, bulbs, fruit trees, etc. You should have ready:

  > items to be planted
  > fertilizer
  > peat moss
  > garden hose and spades (include small spades for children)

- Pick and prepare fruit or garden produce.

- Can, preserve, or freeze fruits and vegetables for winter:

  > make apple butter, grape jam, peach preserves
  > can green beans, tomatoes, beets, etc.
  > freeze corn, squash, cherries, berries

Remember to include small children. They can shell peas, wash jars, snap beans, pick up boxes of wood chips, water plants, etc.

MEMORIES / KEEP ALIVE

MEMORIES / KEEP ALIVE

VIDEO VIRTUOSOS

If there is a video camera in the family, work together to create a TV pilot film. Brainstorm to come up with a plot. Then write a script; assign family members, old and young, to play the parts. You might need the following:

> a writer
> a producer
> a director
> a camera operator
> actors
> costume coordinator
> makeup artist
> technical director (who sees to details like providing fresh power packs, supplying cool drinks for actors, running errands, etc.
> a VCR to replay your masterpiece

Don't be afraid to let children take part in all these areas. They are very creative at inventing plots and often know a great deal about television production.

Your show might be a mystery, drama, situation comedy, quiz show, or talk show. You will probably need to proceed with the following steps:

- Create a script.

- Block out the scenes and scout the filming locations.

- Rehearse each scene.

- Film scenes in sequence (unless your equipment has editing capabilities).

To assure the success of this project, relax and have fun. Don't be afraid to try something crazy. The adults should not be too exacting or critical; remember, the idea is to "make a memory" that is *fun* for everyone.

LITERARY HERITAGE

Spend a rainy afternoon with the books and records you loved as you (or your children) were growing up. Play records of songs or stories; take turns reading little storybooks aloud, recalling events associated in your minds with those books or records. The little ones of the third generation will love this time, too.

Reread aloud as a family the great children's literature that has allegorical meaning to you now. Discuss the spiritual or moral applications that you now understand as an adult.

BOOKS

Love You Forever by Robert Munsch
The Chronicles of Narnia by C. S. Lewis
Alice in Wonderland by Lewis Carroll
The Giving Tree by Shel Silverstein
Hope for the Flowers by Trina Paulus
Tom Sawyer and *Huckleberry Finn* by Mark Twain
Treasure Island by Robert Louis Stevenson
The Velveteen Rabbit by Margery Williams

NURSERY RHYMES AND POEMS

"There Was a Crooked Man," attributed to Mother Goose
"Mary Had a Little Lamb" by Sarah Josepha Hale
"Pussy Cat, Pussy Cat" by Christina Rossetti
"The Duel" by Eugene Field
"Swing Song" by William Allingham
"The Owl and the Pussycat" by Edward Lear

POETRY

"Thanatopsis" by William Cullen Bryant
"The Landing of the Pilgrim Fathers in New England" by Felicia Hemans
"A Thing of Beauty" by John Keats
"If" by Rudyard Kipling
"The Eternal Goodness" by John Greenleaf Whittier
The poems of Robert Louis Stevenson
"Two Roads" and "Stopping by Woods on a Snowy Evening" by Robert Frost
Poems by Henry Wadsworth Longfellow such as:
   "The Wreck of the Hesperus"
   "Psalm of Life"
   "Song of Hiawatha"
   "The Village Blacksmith"
   "I Heard the Bells on Christmas Day"

MEMORIES / KEEP ALIVE

MEMORY BOOK

Rather than keeping a "baby book," keep a Memory Book. Buy a blank book for each child and keep a sort of diary of that child's growth: physical, emotional, spiritual. Every few months (or weeks, if the child is very young) make an entry. You might include:

how they have grown
things they have learned
special experiences (bad moments as well as good moments)
how you felt about those moments
why that child is special
new events or things that are going on in the world at that time
special things the child says
special awards or honors, relating the event as a special family time

Give the book (or books) to the child as a gift when he or she is old enough to appreciate it. Some occasions for this gift might be:

sixteenth birthday
eighteenth birthday
high school graduation
college graduation
wedding day

SCRAPBOOK

Keep a scrapbook for each child in the family. Begin at birth and maintain it as long as possible. Include:

- Pictures as they grow.

- A picture of your house when the child was born (years later, the house will have changed—it might be a new color; additions may have been built; trees will have grown; etc.).

- Snapshots to show what parents, grandparents, siblings, cousins looked like when the child was born.

- Pictures of the child's first room or nursery.

- Written paragraphs of cute things he or she said, accounts of accidents and experiences.

- Pictures of holidays and memorable moments:

  first lost tooth
  first haircut
  first day of school
  first pumpkin carved for Halloween
  piano recitals, sports participation,
      speeches made
  news clippings
  original writing (stories, poems, etc.)
  best art effort at each age (if not drawing,
      take photos of sculptures, drama,
      craft items, etc.)

MEMORIES / KEEP ALIVE

DANAE—THE APPLE OF OUR EYE . . .

When I was carrying our first child, my mother-in-law told me to expect a boy because, historically, the Dobsons rarely produced little girls. Jokingly she said she didn't think she'd even know *how* to care for a granddaughter. Jim was also expecting a boy, reminding me that six families in his parents' generation had borne only one female among many males. This made me want a little girl all the more. However, I decorated the nursery in yellow and white just to be safe.

Needless to say, we were delighted when our daughter, Danae, was born. Jim's mom was equally pleased (and yes, she learned how to take care of little girls remarkably well!).

Danae's early childhood was so exciting for Jim and me as we watched the development of our creative and happy daughter. We lived on the most fertile street in Southern California, and an array of children incessantly knocked on our front door to play with Danae.

One day when she was about four years old, I decided to give Danae and her friends a tea party. I got out my special china from the cupboard and we planned a party complete with cookies and napkins. Danae helped me create pretend names for all her friends. There were Mrs. Perry, Mrs. White, Mrs. Green, and I was Mrs. Snail (I didn't ask any questions!). The names stuck and every time we decided to have a tea party in the future, I was Mrs. Snail.

Danae had always had a soft place in her heart for animals, whether real or stuffed. As a small child, she would place her dolls on a shelf, and role-play with her teddy bears, stuffed rabbits, and kittens. Each one had a special name and would take its turn sleeping with her. She has grown up to be a fine young woman, now living away from home, and her furry friends are stored away in her keepsake box, silent reminders of the precious childhood that is now history.

I admit that it has been difficult for me to see Danae grow up. Oh, I know that she could not remain a child, and I wouldn't want to freeze her development at an immature age. But I loved every minute of her childhood and cherish the memories we created during those happy years.

I worked especially hard on the task of "letting go" of Danae during her last three years at home. Sometimes that involved the most difficult assignment

of all: permitting her to experience the painful consequences of irresponsibility and immaturity.

One such incident occurred when she was fifteen years of age. Danae had stayed up far too late one night and then could not pull herself out of bed the next morning. This had happened several times before, and each time I had rescued her by helping get things together and then driving her to school. Jim and I agreed, however, that it was time for Danae to accept *full* responsibility for getting to school before the tardy bell rang.

On this particular morning, Danae was running hopelessly behind. When her carpool ride arrived and the driver honked, she came flying out of the shower, draped in a towel, and asked me if I'd please wave them on—she wasn't going to make it. Quite obviously! I stuck my head out the door and gave them the "good-bye" sign. I was involved in a class at that time myself and was in the process of getting ready to leave.

In approximately forty-five minutes, with bed made and the bathroom straight, a beautifully groomed fifteen-year-old appeared at my door and said, "Uh . . . Mom, it's almost time for my algebra class. I can't walk because these shoes hurt my feet."

I ignored the hint and said, "Well, take them off and put on your tennis shoes and just before you get to school, switch back."

"Oh, Mother!" she said. "I couldn't do that. Do you realize how ridiculous this pleated skirt would look with tennis shoes?"

I said, "Well, I guess you have a problem then," and continued combing my hair.

Danae said, "Do you think I could make it on time if I rode Ryan's skateboard to school?"

Now, she and I both knew that there was no way she intended to ride her ten-year-old brother's skateboard to school. A sophomore in high school arriving at school on a skateboard was unheard-of. She would have suffered a barrage of adolescent ridicule from her classmates. She was hoping that I would weaken and drive her to school. Nevertheless, I responded to her proposal as if she were serious. Casually I said, "Danae, it wouldn't matter what you rode to school, you couldn't make it in ten minutes. Besides, you'd better check with Ryan before you borrow his skateboard."

She turned around with a "woe is me" look on her face and walked away. Pretty soon I heard her shuffling down the hall again.

"Uh . . . Mom, how much do you think it would cost to get Dial-a-ride out here?" (Dial-a-ride is the name of our city-sponsored cab company.)

I said, "I don't know, Danae. You'll have to check it out."

She made a hasty call and then returned to say, "Good! It's only 75 cents and Dad owes me a dollar on my allowance. They'll be here in ten minutes."

Danae gathered up her books and went out in front of the house and sat on the curb with her head down, waiting for Dial-a-ride. I was then faced with one of the most difficult assignments I've experienced. I backed my car out of the driveway and left my beloved teen-age daughter sitting dejectedly on a curb. As I drove off, my mind was flooded with all the horrible things that can happen to a young girl sitting alone on the edge of a street: what if the cab driver never took her to school, and other similar thoughts. I lifted my teary eyes up to my heavenly Father and I said, "Lord, You know I'm trying to be a good parent. I'm hoping to teach Danae responsibility through this experience, but it's so difficult. Would You send a guardian angel to watch over her and get her to school safely?"

The Lord heard my prayer, for she came bounding into the house after school, threw her books on the table, flung herself across the counter and wailed, "Oh, Mother! How embarrassing! How horrible! Do you know what kind of cab Dial-a-ride has? It is a huge, *old, beat-up station wagon*. The driver drove me right up in front of the school and all my friends saw me. Oh (groan), I will never do that again!" (Ah, poetic justice.)

Not risking another disastrous episode, Danae was up at the crack of dawn the next morning with the shower blasting. We both profited from the stresses of that encounter with irresponsibility.

It is extremely difficult for loving, caring parents to let their vulnerable kids face embarrassment or failure—especially when they could so easily "bail them out" in moments of irresponsibility. Nevertheless, there is value to be derived from painful or stressful consequences. Even the inevitable conflict that occurs between adolescent and parent can be beneficial. I remember bumping heads with Danae later that same year over a bad

attitude that she was revealing. We stood toe to toe and flung harsh accusations at one another, followed by guilt (mine) and further rebellion (hers). I felt like I had "blown it" to let my emotions get so out of control, and left in the car to run some errands.

When I returned, I found a chocolate cake Danae had baked. Beside it was a note which read, "I'm sorry I was so difficult to get along with today, Mom. This cake is for you." A little love goes a long way to ease the pain of a frustrated mother. We ate the cake together and talked about how we could do better in the future.

The writer of the book of Hebrews fully understood the function of distress and even punishment in shaping our lives and helping us grow. It is beautifully stated in chapter 12, verses 7–11 (TLB):

Let God train you, for he is doing what any loving father does for his children. Whoever heard of a son who was never corrected? If God doesn't punish you when you need it, as other fathers punish their sons, then it means that you aren't really God's son at all—that you don't really belong in his family. Since we respect our fathers here on earth, though they punish us, should we not all the more cheerfully submit to God's training so that we can begin really to live?

Our earthly fathers trained us for a few brief years, doing the best for us that they knew how, but God's correction is always right and for our best good, that we may share his holiness. Being punished isn't enjoyable while it is happening—it hurts! But afterwards we can see the result, a quiet growth in grace and character.

FAMILY BULLETIN BOARD

Hang a family bulletin board in your kitchen, family room, or hallway. Each family member should have a section in which to share his or her:

achievements
talents
messages
snapshots

You might want to work together as a family on special seasonal displays:

Christmas
Valentine's Day
autumn collages

CHRISTMAS AMBROSIA

A traditional Christmas dish for many families is ambrosia. Often each of five different family units brings one ingredient and each family chooses one member to put that family's contribution into the ambrosia bowl. If you have only two or three grown children, make up the other three ingredients by inviting an aunt and uncle, grandparent, or a neighbor to share in this special recipe. For the Dobson family's ambrosia recipe, see page 61.

Combine equal amounts of:

    snowflake coconut
    pineapple tidbits
    tiny marshmallows
    mandarin oranges (canned)
    seedless green grapes

The host mixes this with sour cream in a proportion of 1 cup sour cream to 10 cups of combined fruit ingredients. You may wish to add English walnuts to the fruit mixture.

MEMORIES / KEEP ALIVE

TAFFY PULL

When the kids (and their kids) are home, have a taffy pull. Since this is such a good winter activity, it is perfect for Thanksgiving or Christmas, or the days after.
See page 114 for a good molasses taffy recipe.

MEMORABLE MEMORY MAKERS

Barbara Johnson

Founder of Spatula Ministries, humorist, and
author (*Stick a Geranium in Your Hat and Be Happy*
and other books)

In our home we had a "grumpy corner," and anyone who came in frowning or surly would get to sit there. The wall was covered with cartoons, jokes, a red panic button, and lots of other FUN things (this was in the days before we had "joy boxes"). Friends would bring me stuff for our grumpy corner until finally the whole wall was full and it had spread out to the rec room. Over the door leading to the rec room was a splotch of hair and what looked like drops of blood with a sign under it that said, "Low Overhead." So many friends and family enjoyed contributing to our grumpy corner that before long we didn't even NEED it because frowns disappeared whenever the frowner saw all the funny stuff.

Another tradition was that I would post the boys' after-school chores in a note on the refrigerator every day, and "sign" it with a big, red lipstick kiss on the bottom. It was our family communication system, and it worked well until one day I came home and found a note typed very amateurishly to David with a HUGE list of chores ranging from bathing the dog and cleaning the pool to washing the car and cleaning the bedrooms. It was signed MOM with a big lipstick kiss on it. It turned out Barney, our youngest son, had typed this long list and then put on my lipstick and kissed the note so David would think it came from me. That fouled up our system temporarily, but we got back on course and the system worked fine as long as Barney didn't type out the list.

With four boys and Bill in the family, sorting all the socks was a big pain for me; they never seemed to pair up right. Finally, in desperation, I would toss all the socks into a big box and let everyone pair up their own. Then Barney, the most money-conscious one, offered to sort the socks if I would pay

him a nickel for every pair. Sounded fair enough for me—until one day I noted he was charging me for more pairs than I had even WASHED! He was putting CLEAN socks in the box and charging me a nickel a pair. That was one tradition that didn't last long!

One of my favorite traditions occurred at Christmastime. Since I come from a small family and married into a smaller one (Bill is an only child) we looked for ways to create large, festive Christmas gatherings. We often invited several families over to sing carols around our player piano, and then we had a Christmas craft or contest for each family after the sing. The favorite was having each family build a gingerbread log cabin. Ahead of time we baked enough long and short "logs," spacer blocks, and sections of roof from gingerbread cookie dough for each family. (You can also use graham crackers.) Then the families worked together to build their own houses, sticking the logs together with powdered-sugar icing (made from 2 cups powdered sugar mixed with 1/4 cup water). When the icing dripped down it gave the cabins an icicle look. The objective was just for everyone to have fun and do something together—and the log cabins tasted good, too!

Barbara Johnson

Claire Cloninger

Songwriter and author (*Postcards from Heaven* and *When God Shines Through*)

The Cloninger Holiday Hat Party

One of my favorite Cloninger traditions is our annual Holiday Hat Party. Held between Christmas and New Year's when all of Spike's siblings and their families gather, it is definitely a festive highlight. Silliness is the order of the day!

Each member of the family spends all day creating a crazy hat, and there is much intrigue as no one is to view another person's hat until the evening unveiling at the actual party itself. There is a great gathering of supplies—everything from construction paper to batteries to the kitchen sink. Anything goes!

At dinner the menu is always the same: chicken and sausage gumbo with lots of salad and French bread and assorted desserts. At the magic hour, guests convene, looking absurd but acting as though nothing is out of the ordinary. During dinner, each guest is invited to give a five-minute speech in support of his or her hat. These are generally hilarious.

During dessert, votes are cast for "Hat of the Year," and after multiple ballots (since everyone votes for his or her own hat on the first ballot), a winner is selected. Flashbulbs are popping as the top three hats are announced. The first-place winner is awarded the traditional hat medallion (a small plastic derby on a satin ribbon), and is made trustee of the "Amazing Hat Scrapbook of Photos." (Some winners I recall were Uncle Curt's elegant candelabra hat with lighted candles, Aunt Vali's edible babushka made entirely of pretzels, and Spike's electric basketball hat.)

The evening is generally "capped off" by a gala hat parade to the strains of the totally original and exceptionally beautiful Hat Party anthem, "Put on a Funny Hat" (written by guess who!).

Believe it or not, this tradition has been in effect in the Cloninger clan for more than twenty-five years and is still going strong! Our children grew up believing that fun has no age limit as they watched parents, grandparents, aunts, and uncles embrace this madcap event with childlike enthusiasm.

Claire Cloninger

Lillie Knauls

Singer, recording artist

My mom did domestic work for one of the bank executives. Each Christmas he would personally deliver a large box of fruit, nuts, and candies to our house.

We were not what you might call a "poor" family; however, my parents did not give anything except practical gifts, and not many of them. They were more interested in having a gathering of the family and friends for a time of fellowship and food (the only time we had "ambrosia"—I LOVE IT!) than the giving and receiving of gifts.

Consequently, I grew up believing that Christmas is Christ's birthday and not a time for going into debt to buy gifts for everyone. I now like to buy and give gifts for no reason.

Lillie Knauls

My wife, Nicki, wrote the following description for the original release of **Let's Make a Memory**. Now Nicki is undoubtedly watching from heaven as we continue this beloved tradition:

One of the traditions our family has carried on from my parents (and hopefully our children will pass it along to their children) is the custom of reading the lovely story of Jesus' birth from the Gospel of Luke before opening our Christmas presents.

Grandparents, sisters, brothers, uncles, aunts, and cousins have all participated in this ritual over the years. Now, both grandfathers are gone, but how fortunate we are to have my father, Pop Crim, and Nicki's father, Pop Dale, on tape reading the Christmas story to the family—which incidentally proved to be their last Christmas with us.

We think it is a beautiful tradition worth passing along to our children.

Mort Crim

Mort Crim

NBC news anchor, WDIV-TV, Detroit

Elisabeth Elliot

Missionary, author, speaker
Widowed when her first husband, Jim Elliot, was
killed by Auca Indians

I am grateful for family "prayers," which we had twice a day. In the morning after breakfast we all (six children and parents) went into the living room and sang a hymn. Either Father or Mother played the piano and we all sang, not skipping stanzas, and moving straight through a hymn book, one hymn per day. As a result of this, all of us know hundreds of great old hymns by heart. There is no calculating the value of this treasury in my own spiritual progress.

Next to the Bible, hymns speak most deeply to my needs and daily experience. In times of great temptation and loneliness (in the jungle, for example) I have been sustained by those wonderful words, etched deeply in my mind in those malleable childhood years. You know how easily your children learn TV commercials. Why not stuff their minds with something much more lasting and profitable? Memorization is a snap for children.

I taught Valerie, my own daughter, hymns when we lived in thatched houses in the jungle, sitting on her bed with her just before she went to sleep. We had no piano, of course, and no family. Sometimes there were Indians around, marveling at the strange "noise" we made. I typed up many hymns from memory when I had no hymn book, and bound some of them in a small booklet for her when she learned to read.

Scripture commands us to "speak to ourselves with psalms and hymns and spiritual songs." A family that sings builds a strong spiritual bond and creates for each individual a priceless source of comfort and godly instruction that will always be there, whether he is in touch with other Christians or in a situation where such fellowship may be impossible.

Elisabeth Elliot

James Dobson

Psychologist, speaker, founder of Focus on the Family, and husband of Shirley Dobson

Shirley and I have given the highest priority to creating and continuing a battery of traditions in our family life. We took up the sport of skiing specifically for this purpose. I have many priceless "video tapes" in my mind of the four of us burning down the mountain on skiis with the sound of laughter echoing from the trees. Every Thanksgiving holiday for twelve years was spent in that way. Another activity that was especially meaningful to me was carried on from my childhood. My father and I loved to hunt and fish together when I was a boy. There is no way to describe what those days meant to me as we entered the woods in the early hours of the morning. How could I get angry at this man who took time to be with me? We had wonderful talks while coming home from a day of laughter and fun in the country.

When our son Ryan turned twelve years of age, I introduced him to the ultimate "guy thing." We hunted rabbits, quail, pheasant and larger game whenever the opportunity afforded. As it was with my father, my son and I have had some wonderful conversations while out in the fields together.

A few years ago, for example, we got up one morning and situated ourselves in a deer blind before the break of day. About twenty yards away from us was a feeder which operated on a timer. At seven A.M., it automatically dropped kernels of corn into a pan below.

Ryan and I huddled together in this blind, talking softly about whatever came to mind. Then through the fog, we saw a beautiful doe emerge silently into the clearing. She took nearly thirty minutes to get to the feeder near where we were hiding.

We had no intention of shooting her, but it was fun to watch this beautiful animal from close range. She was extremely wary, sniffing the air and listening for the sounds of danger. Finally, she inched her way to the feeder, still looking around skittishly as though sensing our presence. Then she ate a quick breakfast and fled.

I whispered to Ryan, "There is something valuable to be learned from what we have just seen. Whenever you come upon a free supply of high quality corn, unexpectedly provided right there in the middle of the forest, be careful. The people who put it there are probably sitting nearby in a blind just waiting to take a shot at you. Keep your eyes and ears open!"

Ryan may not always remember that advice, but I will. It isn't often a father says something that he considers profound to his teenage son. One thing is certain: This interchange and the other ideas we shared on that day would not have occurred at home. Opportunities for that kind of communication have to be created. And it's worth working to achieve.

Corrie ten Boom (1892–1983)

World-famous speaker and author (*The Hiding Place, Tramp for the Lord,* and others)

My security was assured in many ways as a child. Every night I would go to the door of my room in my nightie and call out "Papa, I'm ready for bed." He would come to my room and pray with me before I went to sleep. I can remember that he always took time with us, and he would tuck the blankets around my shoulders very carefully, with his own characteristic precision. Then he would put his hand gently on my face and say, "Sleep well, Corrie . . . I love you."

I would be very, very still, because I thought that if I moved I might lose the touch of his hand; I wanted to feel it until I fell asleep.

Many years later in a concentration camp in Germany, I sometimes remembered the feeling of my father's hand on my face. When I was lying beside Betsie on a wretched, dirty mattress in that dehumanizing prison, I would say, "Oh, Lord, let me feel Your hand upon me . . . may I creep under the shadow of Your wings."

In the midst of that suffering was my heavenly Father's security.

From Corrie ten Boom, *In My Father's House* (Fleming H. Revell, a division of Baker Book House, © 1976), p. 58. Used by permission.

As my grandparents gathered their children around the table for meals, one of them read from the Bible, usually three times a day. It was kind of spiritual dessert. They had enjoyed physical food from the hand of God; now they would enjoy spiritual food.

My father was one of those children. Later, when four small offspring sat around his table, he initiated the same practice. (As far as I know, his brothers and sisters have done similarly in their homes.) We never discussed whether or not we wanted to do this; it was just always done and never, to my knowledge, questioned. Reading material was chosen according to our ages. Often at the evening meal we read from a Bible storybook, but at least once a day we read short selections from the Bible. For some reason we read Proverbs more than any other single book; my parents must have believed that book contained an extraordinary amount of wisdom for everyday living.

To the children in our family this was a logical thing for a Christian family to do. No one left the table, unless for special reasons, until we read the Scriptures together. This was no legalistic ritual; it was family habit. Thinking back, I remember numerous instances when our friends called for us and we asked them to wait until we had finished dinner. Dessert may have been served, but none of us ever considered the meal finished until we had read together.

Taken from the book, *Honey for a Child's Heart* by Gladys Hunt. Copyright © 1969 by Zondervan Publishing House. Used by permission of Zondervan Publishing House.

Gladys Hunt

Author of *MS Means Myself, Honey for a Child's Heart, Does Anyone Here Know God?* and others

Karen Mains

Author of *Open Heart, Open Home* and wife of
David Mains, pastor of "Chapel of the Air"

One tradition that marks the David Mains family clan is an insistence on evaluation. We rarely attend any media function or performance, whether it be a concert, the theatre, or just an evening of television, without asking ourselves and the children to rate the experience. David invariably asks, "Well, how do you rate it? What number do you give it, from 1 to 10?"

The purpose of all this is not to raise snobbish critics, but to develop a healthy sense of evaluation in ourselves as well as the children in order that we and they may not be helpless in the face of the incredible media bombardment of the secular generation.

Once we have given our number rating, we share together the reasons why we have picked 3 or 7 or 10. At this point much discussion ensues, which encourages the idea process in grade-schoolers as well as teens. We want the children to know why they have attended certain functions or why not. What was the value of specific events, or why was it valueless? What were the world-views of the directors, creators, and participants?

The children are learning that Christian thinking demands a Christian philosophy of viewing. There are some (really, many) events we deny ourselves because of that developing philosophy. They are either too banal to deserve our time or too tawdry to involve our spirits. We feel that Christians must learn to evaluate what they see, and we feel that we are giving the children a tool that will protect them against this media world. They are developing spiritual defenses and are learning to approve the excellent and to recognize what is honorable, just, pure, lovely, gracious, or worthy of praise.

Karen Burton Mains

Dede Robertson

Author of *My God Will Supply* and wife of Pat Robertson, founder of the Christian Broadcasting Network and host of "700 Club"

Christmas Eve at the Robertsons' centers around the birth of our Savior, Jesus. There is a lovely old crèche (a manger scene), which was given to me by my aunt and uncle the year I discovered there was no Santa Claus. The stable is made of window-shade rollers and slats (their business enterprise). The figures are made of delicately painted German porcelain. All have survived many moves and even a fire with only a few lost sheep and some broken heads, which were easily repaired with Elmer's Glue.

Dressing the house in its Christmas finery is a family thing, with the boys cutting the green boughs and holly, and Pat often joining in on the search for the perfect tree, its cutting, and final stand. The manger scene is set up without the baby Jesus, and all lies in readiness for Christmas Eve. After a traditional supper (traditional since living in Tidewater, Virginia) of scalloped oysters, chicken salad, hot ham biscuits, cranberry orange ring, and orange date nut bread, we gather around the piano singing Christmas carols and sharing with one another. Soon Pat picks up a Bible or has one of the children bring him one. This is the signal for us all to gather around him at the crèche.

Turning to Luke 2, Pat reads that beautiful account of the very first Christmas—the birth of our Savior, Jesus Christ. The children are encouraged to share what this means to them. Pat leads us all in a prayer of thanksgiving for God's love and God's willing sacrifice of His precious Son for each one of us.

Then—the big moment—the youngest child, who knows where He is hidden, has the privilege of placing the baby Jesus in the manger. The first to do this was Tim, who quickly surrendered to Elizabeth, then Gordon, who later surrendered to Ann, who has carried on the tradition until the grandchildren appeared on the scene. Now, they are passing on the tradition.

What a joy to watch the little ones' eyes light up, to see the tender care that is given to the proper placement of the tiny figurine, and to see the bright shining eyes of the others as they watch breathlessly to make sure it is properly done. A tradition, yes, even a ritual, but one that has helped to instill the all-encompassing love of God for each one.

Sincerely,

Dede Robertson

Wayne Watson

Contemporary Christian vocalist and author of
Watercolour Ponies

We aren't a traditional family. It's taken me years to realize and admit that! But memories? Mental **boxcars** full! Many of those memories are of very specific happenings in our lives . . . most of which only happened once but will never, ever be forgotten. By this we've learned that sheer repetition, alone, does not make a memory.

Once we put together gifts for the homeless in downtown Houston as a family. We'll never forget that; it was something we felt especially compelled to do one particularly cold Christmas. Another memory is the time Adam and I had a little accident in our boat. It really rattled me and showed him a side of Dad he'd never seen before. I've also traveled quite a bit with the boys. I've taken both of them to Washington and other cities, just the two of us, on trips that were full of memories—some as petty as leaving our camera full of shots in the Capitol building!

But not all memories come from specific occasions. Memories are made every day in families where people love each other. The very definition of the word **love** launches a million different variations of life and the memory of it.

Compassion within a family will turn outward as you and your family encounter people in need. Let your Christ-likeness show as a family (perhaps without anyone else knowing . . . that is, don't crow about it). Discuss ways to reach out in your little corner of the world to those who may be a little down and out. That will be a memory that will go beyond the boundaries of your own home.

Forgiveness can make a memory as you stumble over each other's feelings in life's journey. Too often, little offenses are forgotten without proper confession and forgiveness. You and your family will hold dear those moments where godliness overcomes humanity. Those places where parents admit failure and a child's eyes are filled with wonder at your honesty are memories to treasure.

Patience added to any task will make a memory. It may not be the kind that gets reported in the paper, but your children will always remember the kindess you show as you endure the "suffering" of letting them live and learn life's lessons at the pace God sets for them.

In other words, let **love** be your byword. Without even trying, memories, some never to be repeated, will be carved into your hearts and lives. They will be warm and rich and will be the color in the adventure that emerges from a walk of faith.

Dorothy Engstrom

Wife of Ted Engstrom, president emeritus of World Vision

We talked to our three children and we have come up with the following list of special memories.

The last day of school in Wheaton, Illinois (while Ted was president of Youth for Christ), I would pick up the children at school and head for Michigan, station wagon packed, including our darling black shaggy dog, Muggs. After driving 150 miles we arrived at Maranatha, Muskegon, Michigan.

At the entrance the boys always let Muggs out so she could race us to the cottage. She always beat us and was always on the top step waiting for us.

We all spent summers at the Maranatha Bible Conference, working, painting, playing, and learning together. Many pictures flash into our minds of camp life together.

For instance, the kids and I covered all the ceilings with egg carton separators. Then with the leftover cartons they built a treehouse and decorated a cave.

We had hung a pink frying pan from a tree limb. We used this as a gong to sound our dinner call, and the kids could hear it all the way down the beach.

One year the boys found an old rowboat with the front end crushed. They named it Sunken Sam. Gordon piled cement slabs in the rear end so the front end with the hole would ride well out of the water. It was quite a sight watching them (Muggs, too) paddling down the channel.

Maranatha made a great impact on the lives of our three children. It's fun to hear them talking, even yet, about those days.

Dorothy Engstrom

Bill Gaither

Songwriter, Christian recording artist, and
husband of Gloria Gaither

My parents, in their quiet, unassertive way, created many memories that showed me what real strength and commitment are all about. The traditions they established for our family had more to do with modeling a way of life rather than creating activities and events.

For example, one "tradition" they taught was the importance of **being there** for a friend or loved one when there was simply nothing else anyone could do. They showed me the importance of **dependability** in a time when there are few things you can really count on. It has made me proud when I've heard people say, "You can always count on George and Lela." They have shown me that in life sometimes we win, sometimes we lose; but more important than winning or losing, is how we react to both of these "impostors," as Kipling called them.

Another "tradition" in our family was old-fashioned **hard work.** My parents helped us appreciate it and understand that without it, nothing great is accomplished. And even if the work sometimes got dull and routine, they taught us to create our own joy and excitement, no matter what the job.

They taught us to be aware of the world around us, to treasure life while we lived it. "This is not the rehearsal," they would say. "It's the real thing." But it was more than a saying for them; it's been their way of life. God has been so good to all of us, and really, we're all living in a bonus situation.

Certainly our family enjoyed the tradition of music. My parents saw that I took piano lessons, and they taped music programs for me when I wasn't at home. (They didn't know at the time that it was illegal to do so.) They drove us kids all over the country to sing in all sorts of churches (it was fun and rewarding, even if we did sing "Every Day Will Be Sunday By and By" in the Seventh Day Adventist Church).

Finally, throughout their lives my parents modeled the tradition of growing old graciously—which is not a small art. Now that I'm in midlife, I hope I can learn to face the next periods of my life with the grace and dignity they have. That is not an easy task, because there is something in human nature that is always asking for more. They have also established a tradition of appreciating the little things in life. From them I learned that a cool, summer evening spent in the swing under the red maple is a gift—a bonus. To be able to raise your own food in your garden is a gift—a bonus. To be able to walk three or four miles every day with your own dog is a gift—a bonus. To be able to get hooked on pro football at the age of seventy and know that a quarterback sneak isn't a bad guy is a gift—a bonus. To enjoy a good meal at Captain D's is a gift—a bonus. I didn't deserve these gifts, these bonuses, but thank God, I was raised in a family with a tradition of enjoying and appreciating them, and I'm very thankful for that.

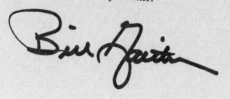

Zig Ziglar

Motivational speaker and author (*See You at the Top!* and others)

I'm not certain this would qualify as a "tradition," but here's what we do in our family and have done for many years.

To start with, my wife (whom I, at her request, lovingly refer to as "The Red Head" when I'm talking **about** her and "Sugar Baby" when I'm talking **to** her—her name is Jean) is known as "The Happy Hugger" because if it's moving she will stop it and hug it, and if it's not moving she will dust it off and sell it. I, too, am affectionate and somewhat of a hugger. For that reason, when I part company with her or come back into her presence, we always embrace each other and express our love for each other. During the course of a day when I'm working around the house—which is where I handle my correspondence, writing, and phone calls—we will often pause and hug. This happens anywhere from ten to as many as thirty times in a single day. They're not long or in any way suggestive hugs; they simply say, "I love you. I'm glad you're mine. I'm glad we're together. You mean a great deal to me."

As a result of this, our three daughters and our son are all affectionate huggers. Not only do they hug us when we greet them, but they also hug each other. Now our three sons-in-law and our daughter-in-law are all in on the act and do a lot of hugging too. Needless to say, our three granddaughters likewise do a considerable amount of hugging.

I believe that from observing many of my acquaintances and associates over the years that, based not only on observation but on their own personal statements, they, too, are getting more into the hugging routine and are expressing their affection more and more. The benefits of hugging are scientifically validated, and the pleasure and enjoyment that comes from it is beyond question.

SEE YOU OVER THE TOP!

Zig Ziglar

Ruth Graham Dienert

Author, daughter of Billy and Ruth Graham.
Works with Samaritan's Purse International

Traditions in a Single-Parent Home

When divorce hits your family, traditions become even more important. But because divorce inevitably leaves a single custodial parent, it also means that keeping up those traditions takes even more effort. The results are worth the effort, however, as you maintain a sense of continuity in a family situation that otherwise may have been torn to shreds.

The one thing that **all** families have is shared histories. Traditions help you remember the happy parts of your family's unique history. Not only is it important to maintain traditions for the children, no matter their age, but also for you, the parent. Your heart and soul also need continuity.

Traditions that I have held on to, and sometimes had to "fight" for, include taking time each day before the children left for school to have a few minutes of Scripture reading and kneeling in prayer. In this way we commit the day and each family member to the Lord. I am also adamant about all of us going to church together as a family.

The holidays provide many opportunities to keep traditions. Choosing and decorating the Christmas tree has always been a family event. Some of the ornaments are twenty-five years old—and look every bit that old—but they are still full of cherished memories. Ornaments the children made in preschool are torn or moldy, but they have a place on the tree. One ornament causes comments each year. It is an eggshell made to look like a baby carriage. I had used it to announce to the children's father that our first child was on her way. And it was used in the same fashion to announce the expectation of the other two who followed. It has long since been crushed, but each year we tenderly take the broken pieces out of the box and smile and remember.

Another tradition the children seem to enjoy is on the night before their birthday, I tuck them in, sit on their bed, and tell them about their birth and how excited I was when they arrived. At each birth, I claimed a Bible promise for the child, and each year I quote that promise to the child as a reminder of God's participation in their lives and their uniqueness. We usually have tears in our eyes when we finish, but they know they were wanted and are cherished.

A tradition we have just started is gathering on my bed while I read out of my journals the cute and funny things they said as toddlers. It causes great laughter and tears, bonding us and making me glad I took the time to write down these priceless things when they were young.

Ruth Graham Dienert

John Trent

Co-author of *The Gift of the Blessing* and other books

The Gift of a Parent's Blessing

Years ago, when our oldest daughter, Kari, was three years old, it took three tries one night to get her to bed. First came stories and prayers. Then a glass of water. Then her blanket had fallen on the floor. Just when we thought she was down for the night, her voice rang down the hallway.

"Night, Mom. Night, Dad. **And don't forget to bless me in the morning!**"

At three years old, Kari was looking forward to something that children have longed for since Old Testament times . . . their parents' "blessing."

For us, it's been a morning event for Kari and her sister, Laura, each day of their lives. Not a ritual. Not something complicated or confusing. Just five simple steps outlined in God's Word.

If you'd like to leave the memory of a blessing in your child's life, then in your own way and words, pattern a specific time, morning or night, when you share five elements with your child. First, **meaningful touch.** In Genesis 27, Isaac (whose son was over forty years!), began his blessing with a hug and kiss before he spoke a word! For you it may be lifting your children onto your lap, holding their hands, or simply laying your hand on their shoulder.

Then comes the **spoken message.** In other words, you put into words a praise or prayer for them that they hear out loud. But what kind of words? Words that **attach high value** to the child. Isaac used a word picture of a field the Lord had blessed to give his son a picture of how valuable he was to him. Children need our appropriate touch and spoken words of love that attach high value to that child. And what's more, those words used to bless can help build a bright, shining future for a child when we use a fourth element of the blessing, **special future.** Children tend to be literalists when their parents speak positive or negative predictions for their life. When we praise a strength they have or pray for God's best for their future, we are giving them this fourth element of the blessing.

And finally, the blessing becomes real when it's linked with **genuine commitment.** A deliberate action of your taking time to say to your child with your touch, words, and attitude, "Of all the kids in the world . . . I'd choose you."

What did Kari receive that next morning? A blessing as old as Abraham but as current as your home or mine. And while the words change each morning, her blessing that particular morning probably went much like this:

> Lord, may You bless Kari today. And may You help her to know how much You love her and know what a wonderful future You have for her. Thank You for how good she is at helping Mom with her sister, Laura, and for how kind and strong she's becoming. And may she always know that we love her, Lord. Amen.

The blessing isn't a formula, but it does have specific ingredients: It's spoken in love. Shared with our hand on hers or our arms around her. And it's inspired by God's love that we desire to communicate to her. That's a recipe to build a positive future in any child's life!

John Trent

Kathie Lee Gifford

Recording artist and co-host of the *Live with Regis
& Kathie Lee* television program

In the early 1960s a doctor suggested that we spend several weeks at the seashore to alleviate some of my sister's asthmatic symptoms. My parents immediately drove to Rehoboth Beach, Delaware, to find an ocean apartment to rent during the coming summer season. While scouting the town, Mom found a charming "gingerbread" house nestled in the pines, but my father noticed a dilapidated old Victorian boarding house with a "for sale" sign hanging precariously on the side of one of its weathered shingles. Ignoring my mother's protests, he asked the realtor to show him the property, only to discover that the exterior was **House Beautiful** compared to the sight before them as they stepped inside. As they rummaged through the forty rooms and eight bathrooms of filth, rotted debris, graffiti, and dead birds, my mother threatened to divorce my father if he took one more step. But, true to form, he kept right on trudging through the mess, even discovering a wonderful secret stairway to the gabled attic!

After purchasing the "Rehoboth Inn," the five of us began our weekend treks during the bitter winter months armed only with small room heaters, buckets of cleaning paraphernalia, paint, and lots of courage. As a family we have been making the same excursion for fifteen years, watching a lonely old weather-beaten inn take on new life. Of course we children were thrilled to pieces about the project and even Mom, courageously battling the mounds of dirt, forgave my father as each new room we tackled took on cleanliness and character.

Today, "Rehoboth Inn," shining, clean, and inviting, functions as a Christian retreat center and beachfront evange-listic headquarters. But, in a very personal way, it stands as a testimony to the hard work, togetherness, and tenacity of a not-so-traditional family that believed, and still believes, that the value of ownership is only realized through the price of equally valuable earnership.

Kathie Lee Gifford

Kathy Peel

Speaker, author (*The Stomach Virus and Other Forms of Family Bonding* and other books), and contributing editor for *Family Circle* magazine

Memories. We talk about them as though we have a choice of whether or not to make them. We act as if the circumstances of life are like disappearing ink—only there for a moment. We forget our children's minds are like computer disks—constantly recording information. Who's to know which memories will be erased and which will be indelibly etched in their minds? Psychologists say it's the unusual or out-of-the-ordinary happenings—good and bad—that form the strongest memories. This means our kids won't remember how many shirts we ironed, how many deals we closed, or if the kitchen floor was clean enough to eat off of. But they'll remember the April Fool's Day when we put an apple in their lunch with a gummy worm coming out of it. And they'll smile when they look at the photo album of the vacation when the whole family climbed a thirteen-thousand-foot peak together.

One particular tradition that's made our teenagers and their friends some great memories is Bill's famous midnight pancake breakfasts. When our oldest son John hit adolescence, Bill and I worried—as many parents do—about where John and his friends would go and what they would do after football games and school dances. There weren't too many alcohol-, smoke-, and trouble-free places to hang out. We remembered the old adage about problems being opportunities in disguise and hit on what has been for us a great idea. Now, after too many football games and dances to count, our teenagers and their friends have congregated at our house. Bill dons his chef's apron and fixes his famous midnight pancake breakfasts. We serve pancakes with seasonal toppings, juice, sausage—all the

fixings. Sometimes these are elaborate events, planned in advance, with appropriate decorations. Sometimes they're more spur of the moment. Sometimes we record the event for posterity with pictures. Our kids know that the fun place to be late on a weekend night is often at home—with their friends all welcome!

There's just something about being able to say, "Remember when . . ." or "That was hilarious!" . . . or "This is the way our family always does it." Common experiences cement a family together. Bill and I decided years go that we'd rather our kids be raised in a house furnished in early garage sale and experiencing fun family memories than in a picture-perfect house full of expensive furniture. When we have the choice of whether to spend our money on an experience—an occasion or vacation—or buy new furniture, we go for the experience. The furniture will get dirty, scratched, torn, and could end up in a garage sale. The family's memories will last forever.

Vonette Bright

Wife of Campus Crusade for Christ founder and president Bill Bright

Practicing Motherhood with a Busy Schedule

I tried to schedule nothing but family activities before or after the children returned from school. I personally picked them up from school rather than assigning someone else to drive them home. This was the time of day that they wanted to talk. If someone else had to drive them home, I would try to be available when they returned, with milk and cookies or some sort of surprise.

I didn't make the children wait for answers or adjust to my schedule any more than was absolutely necessary. When we had guests and one of the children walked into the room, I taught them not to interrupt the conversation. As soon as possible, however, I stopped the conversation to meet the child's need rather than making him adjust to company. In no way did I want the boys to feel second to our ministry.

Probably the greatest tradition in our family has been family devotions. Nightly we have gathered as a family for Bible reading, prayer, and many family discussions. Whenever Bill was away, he tried to arrange his telephone calls to the office (our home phone connects to the same switchboard) when we would be together, usually just before bedtime. We prayed together as a family, even over the phone. For overseas

calls, of course, our prayers were very brief! We found this devotional time extremely important. Praying together was a help in keeping communication lines clear, and we learned to pray for God's will in our lives—not just what Father, Mother, and the children wanted. Now that the children are grown, I think this is one of the traditions they appreciate most.

Vonette Z. Bright

Sandi Patty

Contemporary Christian vocalist

Many of my childhood memories came from the time my family lived in Phoenix, Arizona. My dad was the minister of music at our church, which kept him very busy—except for Saturdays. Saturday was always the family day, and I can remember every Saturday waking up very early and piling in the car with Mom, Dad, and my two brothers and off we went to the desert for breakfast! Yes, breakfast. Dad would bring eggs, bacon, potatoes, bread, coffee, skillet, and anything else you might need for breakfast on the desert. Once we got there, Dad wouldn't let any of us, including Mom, do anything. He cooked the entire breakfast. He built a fire, fried the eggs, bacon, and potatoes, and we had a feast. My dad was pretty special, and ya' know what? I think breakfast is still my favorite meal!

Sandi Patty

Here are a few things that have been special in our home:

We begin the day together with a well-balanced meal along with prayer and some spiritual food. We also conclude the day with prayer, and the day's activities are shared. This is done as a family or on an individual basis, depending on time schedules.

We emphasize birthdays with the favorite family dinner and gift giving with a cake and ice cream dessert. Friends and family are quite often included in this celebration.

Gift giving is minimized at Christmas time in order to focus our thoughts on the Lord Jesus Christ.

We try to attend, as a family, such activities as Little League games, musicals, school open house, school ball games, recitals, etc. To teach mutual interest in one another is a priority in our home. My husband's conviction in regard to this principle is evident by his frequently setting aside pressing responsibilities in order to be with his family.

My best regards,

Mrs. John MacArthur

Mrs. John MacArthur

Author of *The Ultimate Priority* and *Jesus' Pattern of Prayer* and wife of John MacArthur, pastor of Grace Community Church, Sun Valley, California

MEMORY-MAKING RESOURCES

Some of the books included in this listing are classics and were originally published decades ago; the dates and publishers shown here reflect, in most cases, the more recent editions. Some of the older titles may be out of print, but if you can find them in a library or used-book store, they're still worth reading.

Especially for Parents and Grandparents

Bauer, Gary. *Our Journey Home.* Dallas: Word, 1992. This book offers practical advice and encouragement for parents striving to bring their children and families back into the forefront of their busy lives and to reestablish a solid core of values in their home.

Benson, Bob. *Laughter in the Walls.* A collection of free verse about family living and personal being. You'll know better how to laugh at yourself, deal with daily family life, and know which moments to cherish.

Campbell, Ross, M.D. *How to Really Love Your Child.* Wheaton, Ill.: Victor Books, 1977. Most parents really do love their children, but do they know how to convey that love to them? Dr. Campbell discusses four crucial ways to relate love to our children.

Dargatz, Jan. *52 Simple Ways to Build Your Child's Self-Esteem and Confidence.* Nashville: Thomas Nelson, 1991. This book gives helpful advice for developing self-confidence, decision-making, manners, basic self-defense, and homemaking skills in children.

Dobson, James C. *Hide or Seek* (new, revised edition). Old Tappan, N.J.: Fleming H. Revell, 1974. Ten strategies for combating the false value systems of our society and for cultivating self-esteem, rather than inferiority, in our children.

————. *The New Dare to Discipline.* Wheaton, Ill.: Tyndale, 1992. Revised and updated, Dr. Dobson offers advice about raising children along with his philosophy of child-rearing.

————. *Raising Teenagers Right.* Wheaton, Ill.: Tyndale, 1988. Dr. Dobson answers common questions parents ask about raising teenagers.

————. *The Strong-Willed Child.* Wheaton, Ill.: Tyndale, 1978. Devoted to the unique needs of the strong-willed child, this thorough book focuses on infancy, childhood, and adolescence. A practical "how-to" book on discipline.

Dobson, James, and Gary Bauer. *Children at Risk.* Dallas: Word, 1990. This book exposes the battlefields between traditional family values and godlessness and secular humanism. It provides ideas for how to preserve the words and values upon which our society was founded.

Doud, Guy. *Molder of Dreams.* Colorado Springs: Focus on the Family, 1990. Guy Doud inspires a close look at the impact our influence has on the lives and hearts of others.

Elliot, Elizabeth. *The Shaping of the Christian Family.* Nashville: Thomas Nelson, 1992. This book illustrates the foundational principles and values necessary to create a Christian home and family.

Endicott, Irene M. *Grandparenting Redefined: Guidance for Today's Changing Family.* Lynnwood, Wash.: Aglow, 1992. Practical information and help for grandparents facing the problems of the nineties with their grandchildren and their children.

Evans, Anthony. *Guiding Your Family in a Misguided World.* Colorado Springs: Focus on the Family, 1991. Parents are encouraged to model genuine values, spiritual depth, and self-discipline to strengthen unity in their families.

Fuller, Cheri. *Helping Your Child Succeed in Public School.* Colorado Springs: Focus on the Family, 1993. This books shows how to help a child excel emotionally, spiritually, and academically while attending a public school.

Gaither, Gloria. *What My Parents Did Right.* Wheaton, Ill.: Tyndale, 1994. Refreshing vitamins for discouraged parents—this is a collection of personal stories by sixty Christian leaders and artists recounting what their parents did *right.*

Graham, Ruth Bell. *Prodigals and Those Who Love Them.* Colorado Springs: Focus on the Family, 1993. This book provides comfort, solace, and hope for parents who love a prodigal child.

Hull, Karen. *The Mommy Book.* Grand Rapids: Zondervan, 1991. Fifty mothers share their insights on spiritual education, discipline, and the special needs of the working mother.

Hunt, Gladys. *Honey for a Child's Heart.* Grand Rapids: Zondervan, 1969. A Christian parent and author directs teachers and parents to the best in books, not just those labeled as Christian, but all good books that are "honey for a child's heart." Contains a useful bibliography.

Jenkins, Jerry. *As You Leave Home.* Colorado Springs: Focus on the Family, 1993. This book advises a child who is leaving home on how to meet difficult challenges.

June, Lee N., ed. *The Black Family, Past, Present, and Future.* Grand Rapids: Zondervan, 1991. Support and help for understanding and strengthening the African-American family.

Kelly, Marguerite, and Ella S. Parsons. *The Mother's Almanac.* Garden City, N.Y.: Doubleday, 1975. A comprehensive guide for loving and living with small children, told from a mother's point of view. Here's a witty, practical approach to motherhood ranging from recipes for homemade baby food to camping out with kindergartners.

Kesler, Jay. *Parents and Teenagers.* Wheaton, Ill.: Victor, 1984. Dr. Kesler helps parents see their need to be lovingly effective while raising kids.

Kuykendall, Carol. *Give Them Wings.* Colorado Springs: Focus on the Family, 1994. This book explores the process of saying good-bye to childhood and launching teenagers into adulthood.

Leman, Kevin. *Keeping Your Family Together When the World Is Falling Apart.* Colorado Springs: Focus on the Family, 1993. This book shows how to preserve a marriage while parenting kids with a minimum of hassle and heartache.

————. *Smart Kids, Stupid Choices.* Ventura, Calif.: Regal, 1987. Kevin Leman addresses peer pressure, friends, sex, drugs, dating, self-esteem, and communication.

Leman, Kevin, and Randy Carlson. *Parent Talk.* Nashville: Thomas Nelson, 1993. Answers and insight for parents faced with the complex questions that arise when trying to nurture healthy children in a not-so-healthy world.

Lush, Jean. *Mothers and Sons: Raising Boys to Be Men.* Tarrytown, N.Y.: Fleming Revell, 1988. Practical advice is given to instill self-control, maturity, and morality in a young boy's life.

Morgan, Elisa. *Chronicles of Childhood.* Colorado Springs: NavPress, 1991. This journal enables a parent to record spiritual memories and to chronicle signs of God's love in the life of a child.

Narramore, Bruce, and Vern Lewis. *Parenting Teens: A Roadmap through the Ages and Stages of Adolescence.* Wheaton, Ill.: Tyndale, 1990.

Nowell, David Z., Ph.D. *Stepparent Is Not a Bad Word.* Nashville: Thomas Nelson, 1994. This book is for young persons trying to understand their responsibilities and places in the blended family.

Ross, Bette M. *Our Special Child: A Parent's Guide to Helping Children with Special Needs Reach Their Potential.* Nashville: Thomas Nelson, 1993. Handicaps and special learning challenges are not easy, but this book offers practical help and encouragement for parents of special children.

Rushford, Patricia. *What Kids Need Most in a Mom.* Ada, Mich.: Revell, 1989. Rushford debunks the myths of "super mom" and evaluates priorities and the importance of growing in the different seasons of life.

Schreur, Jack, and Jerry Schreur. *Family Fears: Overcoming the Worries That Threaten Our Families.* Wheaton, Ill.: Victor Books, 1994. How you can stop the cycle of paralyzing worry and embrace the hope and joy Christ has for your family.

————. *Creative Grandparenting.* Grand Rapids, Mich.: Discovery House, 1992. Great ideas and insights for grandparents who are very involved in the lives of their grandchildren.

Smalley, Gary. *The Key to Your Child's Heart.* Dallas: Word, 1992. Proven steps that will help you raise motivated, obedient, and loving children.

Smalley, Gary, and John Trent. *The Hidden Value of a Man.* Colorado Springs: Focus on the Family, 1992. This book challenges men to become loving leaders of their families.

Sullivan, S. Adams. *The Father's Almanac.* Garden City, N.Y.: Doubleday, 1980. An absolutely practical resource for fathers, including everything from how to be a good expectant father to hobo recipes for father-child campouts.

Swindell, Bill. *Fathers, Come Home: A Wake-up Call for Busy Dads.* South Bend, Ind.: Greenlawn Press, 1992. Children need fathers more than a few minutes a day. A call to refocus values and priorities.

Wangerin, Walter. *Little Lamb, Who Made Thee? A Book about Parents and Children.* Grand Rapids: Zondervan, 1993. Stories and essays portray children, teenagers, adults, and parents as they grapple with the deep realities of life.

Weber, Linda. *Mom, You're Incredible.* Colorado Springs: Focus on the Family, 1994. Sharing stories from mothers who have struggled through difficult circumstances, Weber communicates the secrets of giving one's family a higher standard of life.

White, Joe. *What Kids Wish Parents Knew.* Sisters, Ore.: Questar, 1991. White provides ideas for things families can do together.

Wright, Norman, and Joyce Wright. *I'll Love You Forever: Accepting Your Child When Your Expectations are Unfulfilled.* Colorado Springs: Focus on the Family, 1993. This encouraging book explores the impact upon parents when children are mentally or physically disabled, have rejected family values, or were lost through death or miscarriage.

Yorkey, Mike, ed. *Raising Them Right.* Colorado Springs: Focus on the Family, 1993. This book reprints articles from *Focus on the Family* magazine dealing with practical, biblical advice on marrriage, family, and child rearing.

————. *The Focus on the Family Guide to Growing a Healthy Marriage.* Colorado Springs: Focus on the Family, 1993. This book is a compilation of articles from *Focus on the Family* magazine dealing with marriage, husbands, wives, families, and family humor.

Worship and Family Time

Arch Read-Aloud Book Series. Saint Louis: Concordia Publishing House, 1983. Delightfully illustrated, inexpensive Bible stories in modern idiom. Some stories are available with records, so children can read on their own.

Baker, Pat. *The Frazzled Mother's Guide to Inner Peace.* Wheaton, Ill.: Tyndale, 1989. A practical guide divided into ten-minute readings—because moms don't have time to read a whole book.

Beckwith, Mary, and Kathi Mills. *A Moment a Day: Practical Devotions for Today's Busy Woman.* Ventura, Calif.: Regal, 1988. Well-know Christian women share how women can use their gifts to serve God by giving to their family and community.

Briscoe, Jill, and Judy Golz. *I Caught a Little, Big Fish.* Ann Arbor, Mich.: Servant, 1994. Offers numerous, practical insights for nurturing your child's faith. Written in conversational style by a mother-daughter team.

Chambers, Oswald. *My Utmost for His Highest.* Nashville: Oliver Nelson, 1992. This well-known, in-depth daily devotional covers all areas of the Christian life.

————. *Prayer, a Holy Occupation.* Ed. Harry Verploeah. Discovery Publications, 1992; distributed by Thomas Nelson. Challenging insights into the highest privilege a human being can accept.

————. *Still Higher for His Highest.* Grand Rapids: Zondervan, 1989. More classic Oswald Chambers meditations for daily worship.

Egermeier, Elsie E. *Egermeier's Bible Story Book.* Anderson, Ind.: Warner Press, 1969. For older children and up to college age. Very well written, thorough, and accurate. The very best of its kind; includes questions and answers.

Family Walk Devotional. Atlanta: Walk Thru the Bible Ministries, 1991. Designed to help parents train children to apply biblical truths to everyday life, this book includes a story, Scripture passage, and question for each day.

Gire, Ken. *Intimate Moments with the Savior* and *Incredible Moments with the Savior.* Grand Rapids: Zondervan, 1990. Also *Instructive Moments with the Savior.* Grand Rapids: Zondervan, 1992. Refreshing insights in short devotions on the moments with Jesus Christ, including Scripture, meditation, and a prayer for each "moment."

Hromas, Roberta. *Fifty-Two Simple Ways to Teach Your Child to Pray.* Nashville: Thomas Nelson, 1991. This book gives practical suggestions on teaching a child how to talk to God.

Hymns for the Family of God. Nashville: Paragon Associates, 1976. A contemporary hymnal with a super selection of songs. Use it in your family devotions or worship time for singing traditional hymns of praise to God or contemporary, upbeat songs. Now available in paperback.

Jenkins, Jerry, ed. *Families: Practical Advice from More than 50 Experts.* Chicago: Moody, 1993. Ideas, experiences, stories, and practical advice from Christian experts on family issues.

Keller, Philip. *A Child's Look at the Twenty-Third Psalm.* New York: Doubleday, 1961. A beautiful description of the relationship between a shepherd and his flock and the parallels between that relationship and the one we have with our Shepherd—God. Written simply enough for children but profound enough for the whole family.

Lindvall, Ella. *The Bible Illustrated for Little Children.* Chicago: Moody, 1991. This illustrated collection of 183 Bible stories includes discussion questions at the end of each story.

Lucado, Max. *No Wonder They Call Him Savior.* Sisters, Ore.: Multnomah, 1986. This book explores the significance of the cross and the sacrifice Christ made on man's behalf.

More Family Walk. Atlanta: Walk Thru the Bible Ministries, 1992. Using character traits and the fruit of the spirit as its topics, each daily devotion includes a story, Scripture passage, and question for parents to use in leading devotions with their children.

Nouwen, Henri J. M. *With Open Hands.* Notre Dame, Ind.: Ave Maria Press, 1972. A beautiful book of poignant words and pictures about openhanded living.

One Year Bible. Wheaton, Ill.: Tyndale, 1987. Each daily reading in this New International Version of the Bible includes a portion from the Old and New Testament, a Psalm, and a Proverb.

Peale, Norman V. *Bible Stories.* New York: Jove Publications. A great way for the whole family to relate the Bible to real life. A delight to read.

Reimer, Kathie. *One Thousand and One Ways to Introduce Your Child to God.* Wheaton, Ill.: Tyndale, 1992. This books shows how to make learning about God part of a child's everyday life.

Swindoll, Charles. *Growing Wise in Family Life.* Sisters, Ore.: Multnomah, 1988. Dr. Swindoll applies the Bible's wisdom to family life.

Taylor, Kenneth. *Stories for the Children's Hour.* Chicago, Ill.: Moody Press, 1968. Ideal for devotions. Dr. Taylor shows your children the value of prayer, the true meaning of friendship, and the importance of honesty, obedience, and kindness.

Ten Boom, Corrie. *Each New Day.* Grand Rapids: Revell, 1977. Each devotional in this collection includes a short reading, a prayer, and a Scripture reading to encourage Christians in a daily walk.

The Family Worship Bible. Nashville: Broadman and Holman, 1991. This New International Version of the Bible has age-appropriate activities, discussion questions, songs, and lessons by leading Christian authors.

Watson, Jean, ed. The Family Library Series, including *Pilgrim's Progress,* and *The Princess and Goblin.* Grand Rapids: Zondervan, 1980. Read-aloud alternatives to television for children eight and older.

Weising, Gwen. *Raising Kids on Purpose for the Fun of It.* Grand Rapids: Baker, 1989. Offers hundreds of practical ideas for turning leisure time into an adventure to build lasting memories.

Books for Family Activities

Arp, Dave, and Claudia Arp. *60 One-Minute Family Builders: Creative Ideas for Family Fun.* Nashville: Thomas Nelson, 1993. Ideas for quick but meaningful ways to nurture a sense of family.

Ball, Karen M., and Karen Thornberg. *Family Traditions That Last a Lifetime.* Wheaton, Ill.: Tyndale, 1993. Practical suggestions for promoting family togetherness from such people as Jim and Shirley Dobson, Leo Buscaglia, Joyce Brothers, and Mother Teresa.

Black, Thom. *Born to Fly.* Grand Rapids: Zondervan, 1994. Full of hands-on tips on how to discover and encourage your child's natural gifts.

Cole, Ann, et al. *I Saw a Purple Cow.* Boston: Little Brown, 1972. Recipes and instructions for more than 100 activities, from fun clay to puppet shows, to help little minds expand by doing, doing, doing!

Farm, Ranch, and Countryside Guide. New York: Adventure Guide, Inc. A super guide to vacations that will let a family really experience life in the country or on a farm or ranch.

Forte, Imogene, and Marjorie Frank. *Puddles and Wings and Grapevine Swings.* Nashville: Incentive Publishing, 1962. Things to make and do with nature's treasures for kids and their grownup friends.

Frank, Marjorie. *I Can Make a Rainbow.* Nashville: Incentive Publications, 1976. Every marvelous idea possible for making, creating, and doing at home and in the classroom. Covers many media. Really indispensable!

Gaither, Bill, and Gloria Gaither. *Family Travel Kit.* Colorado Springs: Focus on the Family, 1992. This kit includes a tape of twenty-two songs, lyrics, an activity book of car games and quizzes, and four reusable wipe-off game cards for travel bingo with markers, all in a snap-together travel bag.

Gaither, Gloria, and Shirley Dobson. *Let's Hide the Word.* Dallas: Word, 1994. Fun ideas to help the whole family learn Scripture and biblical principles and relate them to life.

Mack, Norman, ed. *Back to Basics.* Pleasantville: N.Y.: Reader's Digest Press, 1961. All the how-to's for building and enjoying traditional American skills—everything from building a barn to constructing a solar-heated water system.

MacKenzie, Joy, and Shirley Bledsoe. *A Big Book of Bible Games and Puzzles.* Grand Rapids: Zondervan, 1982. Bible games and puzzles for kids to enjoy with little or no assistance from grown-up friends. Great learn-and-do stuff for travel, rainy-day, or sick-bed use. (Also a super way to entertain a "wiggler" in long adult-centered meetings.)

Peel, Kathy, and Joy Mahaffey. *A Mother's Manual for Schoolday Survival.* Colorado Springs: Focus on the Family, 1990. This manual includes contacts and charts to help make the school day run smoother.

———. *A Mother's Manual for Summer Survival.* Colorado Springs: Focus on the Family, 1989. This kid-tested manual helps organize summer activities so that summer vacation will be a celebration rather than a harrowing, sanity-threatening ordeal for parents.

Peel, Kathy, and Judie Byrd. *A Mother's Manual for Holiday Survival.* Colorado Springs: Focus on the Family, 1991. This book contains a one-year supply of celebrations to transform mundane moments into magnificent memories.

Simpson, Norman T., ed. *Country Inns and Back Roads (North American).* Stockbridge, Mass.: The Berkshire Traveller Press, 1991. A listing of special, out-of-the-way places in the United States that still have charm and tranquility, including great family-award inns with home-cooked meals and quaint places to stay.

Wigginton, Eliot, ed. Foxfire Series. New York: Doubleday, 1980–1991. What started as a study about the nearly lost customs of early life in America and the mountain folk has become a series of intriguing handbooks on simple living and how to do everything.

The kitchen is a great place for family warmth and communication. Here are a couple of fun cookbooks for kids and the whole family:

Betty Crocker's Cookbook for Boys and Girls. New York: Western Publishing, 1975. A bright, colorful book of fun-filled foods kids can make.

Wilson, Mimi, and Mary Beth Lagerborg. *Once-A-Month Cooking.* Colorado Springs: Focus on the Family, 1992. This book provides an easy plan to prepare two weeks or a whole month of main-meal dishes at one time. It helps busy mothers organize their lives so they can have more time with their families.

Young Children (to age ten)

Many of these titles are excellent for the whole family.

Alcott, Louisa May. *Little Women.* New York: Knopf, 1988. The story of four New England sisters. Their day-to-day life, their quarrels, ambitions, and loves as they grow up are related at a rollicking pace with warm understanding.

Aliki. *Keep Your Mouth Closed, Dear.* New York: Dial Press, 1966. Great fun for children (and for grownups who get to read them!)

Berry, Michael, and Nora Berry. *Seek and Ye Shall Find New Testament.* Irving, Tex.: HSH Educational Media Company, 1992. This find "Waldo"-type book has children searching through pictures of Bible stories for Alex and Abby, the angel twins.

Caswell, Helen. Growing in Faith Library Series. Nashville: Abingdon Press, 1989.

Davis, Katherine. *The Little Drummer Boy.* New York: Macmillan, 1968. One of America's favorite Christmas songs forms the text of a beautifully illustrated children's book. Music is printed at the end of the book.

Dobson, Danae. Forest Friends Series. Dallas: Word, 1992. Eric Martin dreams about adventures with animals in the Big Green Forest where children learn sharing, truthfulness, and caring. These books are for children ages two through five.

———. The Woof Series. Dallas: Word, 1993. Woof, a stray mutt, gives the Peterson children opportunities to learn more about God's ways. These books are for ages five through nine.

Farley, Walter. *Black Stallion.* New York: Random House, 1941. A beautiful story about a boy's love for his horse and the strange understanding that grows between them.

Friends with God Series. Cincinnati: Standard Publishing. Books written for small children about God's teachings.

Gire, Ken. *Adventures in the Big Thicket.* Colorado Springs: Focus on the Family, 1990. This delightful collection of fourteen Aesop's fable-style stories features animal characters from a southern bayou who teach Solomon's proverbs.

Happy Day Books. Cincinnati: Standard Publishing. Christian principles to be taught to children.

Hartman, Bob. Really Reading Series. Grand Rapids: Zondervan. Favorite children's Bible stories written for beginner readers.

Joslin, Sesyle. *What Do You Say, Dear?* New York: HarperCollins, 1986. A children's classic on manners, written with great humor.

Kennedy, Pamela. *The Cotton Tale Books.* Colorado Springs: Focus on the Family, 1990–1992. These board books are for ages two through four.

Keone, Glen. Parables for Kids Series. Elgin, Ill.: David C. Cook/Chariot Books. Stories that help your children apply the Bible to life.

Lucado, Max. *Just in Case You Ever Wonder.* Dallas: Word, 1992. A parent tells a child how special she is to her parents and God. For ages three through eight.

Learn to Read Series. Grand Rapids: Zondervan, 1993. Books about God, written for children.

Lionni, Leo. *Alexander, the Wind-up Mouse.* New York: Pinwheel Books, 1969. Sure to provoke a discussion about being glad you are you.

———. *Frederick.* New York: Pinwheel Books, 1966. We are not alike. We do not all do the same kind of work. Our world needs more than food and material things. Men (and mice) do not live by bread alone.

———. *Swimmy.* New York: Pinwheel books, 1963. A story about how a smart little fish turned the oddity of being different into the blessing of being special by working closely together with others.

———. *Tico and the Golden Wings.* New York: Knopf, 1975. Giving away outward treasures helps us to store up treasures on the inside. Real riches are kept where no one can see.

Norton, Mary. *The Borrowers.* New York: Harcourt, Brace, Jovanovich, 1965. A classic children's story about some "miniature" people and the house they live in.

Searle-Barnes, Bonita. The Wonder of God's World Series. Batavia, Ill.: Lion Publishing. Several titles about God's creation, beautifully illustrated.

Dr. Seuss. *My Book about Me.* Westminster, Md.: Beginner Publications, 1969. Helpful, simple, and delightful for building good self-images in young children.

Silverstein, Shel. *The Giving Tree.* New York: Harper and Row, 1964. A parable about giving and taking; one of the most meaningful books ever for children and grown-ups.

———. *Where the Sidewalk Ends: Poems and Drawings.* New York: Harper and Row, 1974. Zany, crazy poems to tickle any kid's funny bone. Some with very serious points under all the giggles.

Spyri, Johanna. *Heidi.* New York: Western Publishing, 1977. The lovable story about a little girl, Heidi, who lives in the Swiss Alps with her grandfather. She is taken by her aunt to the city for school, but pines for her grandfather and the beauty and fresh air of the mountains, and is finally reunited with her grandfather.

Stevenson, Robert Louis. *Treasure Island.* New York: Ace Books, 1979. Always a favorite, especially with boys. Swiftly moving action from beginning to end. For the most part, the story is told in the first person by the boy hero, Jim Hawkins.

Taylor, Kenneth. The Kenneth Taylor Series. Wheaton, Ill.: Tyndale, 1989–1991. Wonderfully illustrated Bible stories for very young children.

Tazewell, Charles. *The Littlest Angel.* Chicago: Children's Press, 1946. A moving Christmas story. Jesus accepts the most humble gifts, even those that may seem shabby compared to others, especially when they are given with love and adoration.

Travers, Pamela. *Mary Poppins.* New York: Harcourt, Brace and World, 1934. A classic in children's literature. Mary Poppins, with her blend of fantasy and nonsense, pervades this book, which is at once poetry and fun and wisdom.

Trent, John. *There's A Duck in My Closet.* Dallas: Word, 1993. This humorous bedtime story turns a closet full of scary "monsters" into a child's own personal zoo.

Turn the Page and See Series. Cincinnati: Standard Publishing. Exciting books for children about God's goodness.

Whaite, Michael. Building Christian Character Series. Elgin, Ill.: David C. Cook/Chariot Books. Books to teach children about Christianity.

White, E. B. *Charlotte's Web.* New York: Harper and Row, 1952. The unforgettable story about the spider, Charlotte, who weaves messages in her webs to save the life of Wilbur the pig.

———. *Stuart Little.* New York: Harper and Row, 1945. An outstanding adventure about a mouse who goes voyaging. Especially great for boys.

———. *Trumpet of the Swan.* New York: Harper and Row, 1973. Louis, a swan born with the handicap of no voice, faces life with courage and a trumpet to win the love of his life.

Wilder, Laura Ingalls. Little House Books. New York: Harper and Row, 1935. The adventures of a pioneer family portraying a warm, loving home.

Williams, Margery. *The Velveteen Rabbit.* New York: Avon, 1982. The story of a stuffed toy, told from the rabbit's point of view, with deep spiritual meanings.

Wyss, Johann Rudolf. *The Swiss Family Robinson.* New York: Ace Books, 1960. A fun account of a family's life on an uninhabited island. The author makes strong points for obedience to parents and love for one's family.

Zolotow, Charlotte. *A Father Like That.* New York: Harper and Row, 1971. A touching story of the kind of father a little, fatherless boy wishes he had. Good for dads to read too.

———. *The Hating Book.* New York: Harper and Row, 1969. The experience of feeling hated and hating in return is a poignant one for a child. Vibrant drawings.

———. *If It Weren't for You.* New York: HarperCollins, 1966. Oh, to be the only child in the family! Life would be so grand—or would it? A humorous and honest portrait of living with a younger brother.

Children (ages eight through twelve)

Bennett, William. *The Book of Virtues.* New York: Simon and Schuster, 1993. This anthology provides works of literature from history that can be used to teach quality character traits.

Bray, Maria Flandreck. Reba Novels Mysteries. Grand Rapids: Zondervan. Fiction series featuring a young girl heroine who solves mysteries.

Brouwer, Sigmund. The Accidental Detectives Series. Grand Rapids: Victor Books, 1990–1994. Team up with Ricky Kidd and his pals for thrilling action, intriguing mystery, and cliff-hanging suspense. For ages eight through twelve.

Doyle, Peter Reese. The Daring Adventure Series. Colorado Springs: Focus on the Family, 1993–1994. For ages ten through sixteen. Every story in this series of nonstop excitement and mystery demonstrates how to trust God in all situations.

Fraser, Wynnette. Mirror Mountain Adventure Series. Elgin, Ill.: David C. Cook/Chariot Books, 1989. Adventure fiction to fill the leisure hours of adolescents and older children with excitement. Great alternative to TV.

Gunn, Robin Jones. The Christy Miller Series. Christy Miller learns many lessons about God's love and the importance of making wise choices. For girls ages twelve through sixteen.

Hall, Kristi. The Julie McGregor Books. Cincinnati: Standard Publishing. Adventure fiction series for girls.

Herndon, Ernest. Eric Sterling Secret Agent Series. Grand Rapids: Zondervan. Mystery fiction for boys.

Hunt, Angela Elwell. Nicki Hallond Mysteries. San Bernardino, Calif.: Here's Life Publications. A six-book Christian mystery series.

Hutchens, Paul. Sugar Creek Gang Series. Chicago: Moody Press. This exciting mystery series includes more than thirty books.

Levene, Nancy Simpson. The Alex Series. Elgin, Ill.: David C. Cook/Chariot Books. A series of books about Alex, a young girl learning—sometimes the hard way—to be a Christian.

———. T. J. Books Series. Elgin, Ill.: David C. Cook/Chariot Books. A series of adventure stories.

Lewis, Beverly. Holly's Heart Series. Grand Rapids: Zondervan. Fiction books for girls.

Lewis, C. S. The Chronicles of Narnia Series. New York: Collier-Macmillian Publishers, 1970. This set of great adventures with allegorical spiritual meanings is as much a "must" for children as *Pilgrim's Progress* is for adults. These are books to intrigue and involve the whole family. Great classics in Christian literature.

Lucado, Max. *Tell Me the Secrets.* Wheaton: Crossway, 1993. Three children meet a retired missionary couple who share the secrets of life.

McCusker, Paul. The Adventures in Odyssey Series. Colorado Springs: Focus on the Family, 1991–1994. Children can read about that exciting land of "Odyssey." For ages ten through fourteen.

Peretti, Frank. The Cooper Kids Adventure Series. Wheaton, Ill.: Crossway Books, 1990. An adventure series written by one of America's most imaginative Christian authors.

Plemons, Marti. Grace Street Kids Series. Cincinnati: Standard Publishing. Each book contains a specific biblical theme and topical theme for today's kids.

Raper, Gayle. East Edge Mysteries. Elgin, Ill.: David C. Cook/Chariot Books. Mystery stories with Christian principles.

Roddy, Lee. The Ladd Family Adventures Series. Colorado Springs: Focus on the Family, 1989–1994. The Ladd family encounters danger, excitement, and intrigue in their adventures that solve sinister plots while learning about God's important lessons. For ages eight through twelve.

Schulte, Elaine. Colton Cousins Adventures Series. Grand Rapids: Zondervan. These stories combine adventure, historical accuracy, and Christian principles.

Seldomridge, Ray, ed. *The Clubhouse Collection.* Colorado Springs: Focus on the Family, 1993. This is a compilation of twenty of the best-loved stories from the *Focus on the Family Clubhouse* magazine. For children ages eight through twelve.

Sorenson, Jane. Katie Hooper Series. Cincinnati: Standard Publishing. Readers will see much of themselves in Katie as she encounters everyday life as a member of her family.

Stahl, Hilda. The Wren House Mystery Series. Elgin, Ill.: David C. Cook/Accent Books. Books for the mystery lover.

———. Wind Rider Books. Wheaton, Ill.: Tyndale. Books for children who love adventure.

Wold, Ann. Choice Adventures Series. Wheaton, Ill.: Tyndale. A Christian adventure series.

Older Children, Teenagers, and Adults

Armstrong, William H. *Sounder.* New York: HarperCollins, 1969. This Newbery Medal Winner is a sensitive, moving novel about a sharecropper's family and their dog, Sounder, as they face the agonies of poverty and injustice with dignity.

Bolton, Martha. *On the Loose, The Cafeteria Lady.* Colorado Springs: Focus on the Family, 1994. In a wacky way, Bolton shows teens how to laugh about common situations they face. For teenage girls.

Bunyan, John. *The Pilgrim's Progress.* Grand Rapids: Zondervan, 1967. This classic is must reading for mature teenagers through adults. Its universality of spiritual appeal is unmatched.

Burns, Jim. *Radically Committed.* Dallas: Word, 1992. This book helps teen leaders develop leadership qualities necessary to make a difference in the world.

———. *Surviving Adolescence.* Dallas: Word, 1990. This humorous look at the important milestones of adolescence offers advice on picking friends, dating, peer pressure, drugs, alcohol, decision-making, and friends.

Buscaglia, Leo. *The Fall of Freddy the Leaf.* New York: Charles B. Slack, 1962. Distributed by Holt, Rinehart, and Winston. For children who have experienced permanent loss and for the grown-ups who would like to help in finding a way to explain it.

Clemens, Samuel L. *The Adventures of Huckleberry Finn.* New York: Dodd, Mead & Co., 1979. In Mark Twain's classic adventure, Huck is every boy who ever lived and also an individual worth knowing. This humorous novel of life on the Mississippi comes close to being America's most popular book.

Davis, Ken. *How to Live with Your Parents without Losing Your Mind.* Grand Rapids: Zondervan, 1988. Teens are challenged to influence their families by allowing Christ to work through them.

———. *I Don't Remember Dropping the Skunk, But I Do Remember Trying to Breathe.* Grand Rapids: Zondervan, 1990. Davis offers amusing advice to teens about self-esteem, getting along with parents, learning to trust God, being responsible with money, and the search for love.

Defoe, Daniel. *Robinson Crusoe.* New York: Bantam, 1961. A classic adventure/romance story about a young man who lives from one adventure to another.

Dobson, James. *Preparing for Adolescence.* Ventura, Calif.: Gospel Light, 1989. Dr. Dobson speaks to pre-teens and teens about self-esteem, peer-pressure, love, sexual purity, emotions, how to know God's will, conflict with parents, and independence.

Dockrey, Karen: *Family Survival Guide.* Wheaton: Victor, 1988. This guide shows teens how to improve their relationships with their parents.

Dorothy Hamilton Books. Scottsdale, Pa.: Herald Press. Great fiction with a moral impact. Especially interesting to boys: *Busboys at Big Bend, Tony Savala, Charco, Jason, Ken's Hideout,* and other titles. Especially interesting to girls: *Neva's Patchwork Pillow, Bittersweet Days, Marl's Mountain, Kerry, The Castle, Linda's Rain Tree* and other titles.

Doud, Guy. *God Loves Me, So What!* Saint Louis: Concordia, 1992. Doud helps teens discover how faith in Christ affects choices, their views of themselves, and relationships.

Doyle, Peter Reese. The Daring Adventure Series. Colorado Springs: Focus on the Family, 1993–1994. Each story demonstrates how to trust God in all situations. For ages ten through sixteen.

Eareckson, Joni, and Steve Estes. *A Step Further.* Grand Rapids: Zondervan, 1980. The journal of becoming, from the author of *Joni.* Great for young people and adults as well.

Frank, Anne. *Anne Frank: Diary of a Young Girl.* New York: Bantam, 1993. The diary of a fourteen-year-old Jewish girl during the last year of her life before being arrested and killed in a Nazi prison camp.

Gunn, Robin Jones. The Christy Miller Series. Christy Miller learns many lessons about God's love and the importance of making wise choices. For ages twelve through sixteen.

Herriot, James. *All Things Bright and Beautiful; All Things Wise and Wonderful; All Creatures Great and Small; The Lord God Made Them All.* New York: Saint Martin's Press and Bantam Books, 1972–1982. The loving, joyful books by a Yorkshire veterinarian about his friends and neighbors both human and animal.

Holmes, Marjorie. *Two from Galilee.* New York: Bantam, 1982. A sensitive novel about the young girl chosen to be the mother of the Messiah, her love for Joseph, God's plan for her, and life itself.

Leech, Bryan, and Swen Sadler. *It Must Have Been McNutt.* Glendale, Calif.: Regal Books. Who's to blame when something happens around your house? It must have been McNutt. Fun and inspiring.

L'Engle, Madeleine. The Austin Family Series. Includes *Meet the Austins, The Young Unicorns,* and *Arm of the Starfish.* New York: Farrar, Strauss, and Giroux. Another series of fiction no teenager should be without. About a loving family of unique persons—warm and adventuresome.

———. The Time Trilogy Series. New York: Farrar, Strauss, & Giroux, 1979. Includes *A Wrinkle in Time, A Wind in the Door,* and *A Swiftly Tilting Planet.* A wonderfully imaginative and exciting series of fiction that has become a young people's classic. No one should grow up without reading these books (Newbery Medal winner).

Lewis, C. S. The Chronicles of Narnia Series. Paperback set of seven books, boxed. New York: Collier-Macmillian Publishers, 1970. These are books to intrigue and involve the whole family.

Lindbergh, Anne M. *Bring Me a Unicorn.* New York: New American Library, 1974. The diary of a young girl as she grows into a young woman, builds relationships at home, and falls in love.

———. *The Unicorn and Other Poems.* New York: Random House, 1972. Lovely poems from a modern visionary.

Littleton, Mark. *Beefin' Up.* Sisters, Ore.: Multnomah, 1990. This devotional for teens covers such themes as popularity, love, temptation, and peer pressure.

Lofts, Norah. *How Far to Bethlehem?* Cutchogue, N.Y.: Buccaneer Books, 1991. A beautiful novel about the three kings whose thirsts and longings led them in search of the reason for their dreams.

Maclay, Elise. *Green Winter: Celebration of Old Age.* New York: Reader's Digest, 1977. A priceless book of poems in celebration of old age. Every young person should thoughtfully read this to better understand that older people are only young people in older bodies.

Miller, Calvin. The Singer Trilogy. Downers Grove, Ill.: InterVarsity, 1980. Includes *The Singer, The Song,* and *The Finale:* three book-length lyric poems that make a poignant mythic retelling of the story of the New Testament.

Paulus, Trina. *Hope for the Flowers.* New York: Paulist Press, 1972. A picture story for all ages about the risk and pain of becoming something special.

Price, Eugenia. *Leave Your Self Alone.* Garden City, N.Y.: Doubleday, 1993. Subtitled "The Paralysis of Analysis," this liberating book encourages us to do serious business with God and ourselves on the grounds of redemption and then to avoid the pitfall of damaging self-focus.

Shedd, Charlie W. *Letters to Karen.* Nashville: Abingdon Press, 1977. Also: *Letters to Philip.* Old Tappan, N.J.: Fleming H. Revell, 1969. Letters about life, love, and marriage from a Christian father to his daughter (for girls) and to his son (for boys). For real understanding, read both books.

Sheldon, Charles. *In His Steps.* New York: Grossett & Dunlap, 1992. A time-honored classic on the adventure of walking "in His steps." A must for young people.

Stephens, Andrea. *Prime Time Devotions for Girls.* Ada, Mich.: Revell, 1991. Andrea shows how to apply biblical principles to issues such as anger, temptation, reputation, friendship, dating, and getting organized.

Swift, Jonathan. *Gulliver's Travels.* Viking Penguin, 1983. A political and social satire aimed at the English people but representing mankind in general and the English Whigs in particular.

Taylor, Kenneth N. *Almost Twelve.* Wheaton, Ill.: Tyndale, 1989. For when it is time to talk about the facts of life. Handled very openly and sensitively. May be read with the child or read by parent and shared.

ten Boom, Corrie. *The Hiding Place.* New York: Bantam, 1984. The story of a Christian family's sacrifice to house and feed Jewish persons: their arrest and imprisonment and the miraculous release of Corrie herself.

Vanauken, Sheldon. *A Severe Mercy.* New York: Harper and Row, 1977. Recipient of the Gold Medallion Award, here is a testimony to life lived at its deepest and of the conquering possibilities of faith and love.

Worley, Mike. *Brand Name Christians.* Grand Rapids: Zondervan, 1988. Upbeat and easy-to-read, these devotions lead junior-high students through Philippians, Colossians, Ephesians, and Galatians.

Wyse, Lois. *I'm Glad You Are My Son.* New York: Doubleday. A collection of word-gifts from a parent to a son.

Christian Living

a Kempis, Thomas. *The Imitation of Christ.* New York: Doubleday, 1976. The timeless classic by a simple monk whose intention is still valid to the modern reader: "Of painting the way by which all would be able to follow Christ's teachings and by so doing to imitate His life."

Anderson, Neil. *Victory Over the Darkness.* Ventura, Calif.: Regal, 1990. Dr. Anderson helps readers discover biblical principles to use as a foundation for victorious Christian living.

Chambers, Oswald. *Daily Thoughts for Disciples.* Grand Rapids: Zondervan, 1976. A year's collection of devotions from the writing of Oswald Chambers, so soul-stirring they will trouble and inspire you.

Christenson, Evelyn. *What Happens When We Pray for Our Families.* Wheaton, Ill.: Victor, 1992. This handbook teaches how to invoke God's involvement in family matters.

———. *What Happens When Women Pray?* Wheaton, Ill.: Victor, 1992. The author gives a thorough approach to methods to develop the practice of prayer.

Colson, Charles. *The Body.* Dallas: Word, 1992. A book that tackles the tough questions troubling Christians about being light in a dark world.

Crabb, Larry. *Finding God.* Grand Rapids: Zondervan, 1993. In a pop-psychology culture, solving our problems has become more important than finding God, but our deepest problem and worst sin is doubting God.

Dobson, James. *When God Doesn't Make Sense.* Wheaton, Ill: Tyndale, 1993. Dr. Dobson offers advice for those who are confused and disillusioned by the trials of life.

Dravecky, Dave, and Jan Dravecky with Ken Gire. *When You Can't Come Back.* Grand Rapids: Zondervan, 1992. Dave and Jan share how their faith grew in the midst of devastating and disorienting circumstances.

Gaither, Bill. *I Almost Missed the Sunset.* Nashville: Thomas Nelson, 1992. A book addressed primarily to men about finding a balance between the practical, tangible demands and the eternal, intangible values of life.

Gaither, Gloria. *Decision Vision.* Anderson, Ind.: Warner Press, 1991. A Christian's approach to making the right choices. Help on making the decisions that bombard our lives daily.

Keller, Phillip. *A Shepherd Looks at Psalm 23.* Grand Rapids: Zondervan, 1976. Also: *A Gardener Looks at the Fruits of the Spirit.* Dallas: Word, 1979. Two books with unusual insight into the broader meanings behind some important spiritual similes.

Lawrence, Brother of the Resurrection. *The Practice of the Presence of God.* Translated by John J. Delaney. New York: Doubleday, 1977. This journal of one man's prayer life forces us to deal with the command of our Lord to "pray without ceasing."

Lindbergh, Anne M. *Gift from the Sea.* New York: Random House, 1978. A classic for women of all ages from a poet and lover of life who dares to search her most secret corners for her true self.

Packer, J. I. *I Want to Be a Christian.* Wheaton, Ill.: Tyndale, 1977. A thinking person's discussion of what it really means and costs to be a Christian.

———. *Knowing God.* Downers Grove, Ill.: InterVarsity, 1973. For persons who want to go beyond knowing about God to really, deeply knowing Him.

Powell, John. *Fully Human, Fully Alive.* Niles, Ill.: Argus, 1976. A book on positioning. All changes in the quality of a person's life must grow out of a change in his vision of reality.

Schaeffer, Francis. *How Should We Then Live?* Wheaton, Ill.: Crossway, 1983. For Christians concerned about the direction secular humanism is taking our society. The author says people are as they think. The choices in the next decade will mold irrevocably the direction of our culture and the lives of our children.

Smith, Hannah W. *The Christian's Secret of a Happy Life.* Uhrichsville, Ohio: Barbour, 1985. The time-tested classic written by an early-American woman in search of wholeness in the Spirit.

Sproul, R. C. *Knowing Scripture.* Downers Grove, Ill.: InterVarsity Press, 1973. Help for Christians who long to dig out the meaning of Scripture for themselves.

Stott, John. *Basic Christianity.* Downers Grove, Ill.: InterVarsity, 1964. The basics of Christianity are explained.

Swindoll, Charles. *Strengthening Your Grip.* Dallas: Word, 1986. Dr. Swindoll shares essential ingredients—priorities, purity, integrity, prayer, leisure—to live in an aimless world.

———. *The Grace Awakening.* Dallas: Word, 1992. Dr. Swindoll shows how God's liberating grace brings spontaneous, creative freedom.

Trueblood, Elton. *A New Man for These Times* and *A Place to Stand.* New York: Harper and Row. Two classics on how to keep the vital balance between head and heart in a complicated and hungry world.

The Christian Marriage

Briscoe, Jill, and Stuart Briscoe. *Pulling Together When You're Pulled Apart.* Grand Rapids: Victor Books, 1990.

Dobson, James. *Emotions: Can You Trust Them?* Ventura, Calif.: Regal, 1984. Dr. Dobson gives practical guidelines to help understand, control, and channel the emotions.

———. *Love for a Lifetime.* Sisters, Ore.: Multnomah, 1993. Written especially for the engaged and newly married, this book highlights the fundamentals of a Christian marriage and reveals the keys to an enduring relationship.

———. *Straight Talk.* Dallas: Word, 1991. Dr. Dobson helps a husband understand what it means to be a man, how to relate to his wife, his role as a Christian father, his emotions and feelings about mid-life, and his personal faith.

———. *What Wives Wish Their Husbands Knew about Women.* Wheaton: Tyndale, 1977. Dr. Dobson identifies the ten main causes of feminine dissatisfaction and unhappiness in the marriage relationship.

Ezell, Lee, and Lela Gilbert. *Iron Jane.* Vine Books, Servant, 1994. This book deals intelligently with the war between the sexes and calls for a lasting, loving ceasefire.

Fields, Doug. *Creative Romance.* Eugene, Ore.: Harvest House, 1991. Fields offers more than three hundred simple, fun ideas to bring romance back into marriage.

Gaither, Gloria, Gigi Graham Tchividjian, and Susan Yates. *Marriage: Questions Women Ask.* Portland, Ore.: Multnomah and *Christianity Today*, 1992. Candid answers to questions most often asked by women over a decade of letters to *Today's Christian Women* magazine.

Hybels, Bill, and Lynne Hybels. *Fit to Be Tied.* Grand Rapids: Zondervan, 1991. The Hybels combine biblical precepts with reality to recommend creative ways to fortify a marriage relationship.

Jenkins, Jerry. *Loving Your Marriage Enough to Protect It.* Chicago: Moody, 1993. Dr. Jenkins shares six hedges he has developed to protect his marriage.

Littauer, Florence. *Wake Up, Women.* Dallas: Word, 1994. For women who are interested in embracing truth and in integrating genuine Christianity with good, common sense.

Littauer, Fred. *Wake Up, Men.* Dallas, Word: 1994. Written for the thinking Christian man who yearns to breathe new life and spirituality into his family life.

Penner, Clifford, and Joyce Penner. *The Gift of Sex: A Guide to Sexual Fulfillment.* Dallas: Word, 1981. A Christian's guide to sexual enjoyment in marriage.

Peterson, J. Allan. *The Myth of the Greener Grass: Affair-Proof Your Marriage.* Wheaton, Ill.: Tyndale, 1991. This book discusses why extramarital affairs happen and tells you how to affair-proof your marriage or overcome an affair that has occurred.

Rainey, Dennis. *Staying Close: Stopping the Natural Drift Toward Isolation.* Dallas: Word, 1989. Ways to strengthen your marriage bonds so they'll never break.

Smalley, Gary, and John Trent. *The Gift of the Blessing* (new edition). Nashville: Thomas Nelson, 1993. The blessing from a father (or lack of it) can deeply affect a son or daughter's life. This book—a must for fathers and their grown children—addresses how to overcome a childhood without a blessing and shows how to communicate a blessing to a child.

———. *The Language of Love.* Colorado Springs: Focus on the Family, 1991. This book explores "emotional word pictures" to help bridge communication gaps with a spouse, children, parents, or co-workers.

———. *The Two Sides of Love.* Colorado Springs: Focus on the Family, 1992. The authors tell ways to balance the hard and soft sides of love to build healthy, fulfilling, rewarding relationships.

Snyder, Chuck, and Barb Snyder. *Incompatibility: Grounds for a Great Marriage.* Sisters, Ore.: Questar, 1988. The Snyders explain how to enrich love, decision-making, teamwork, and parenting with your partner.

Stoop, David, and Jan Stoop. *The Intimacy Factor.* Nashville: Thomas Nelson, 1994.

Swihart, Judson. *How Do You Say "I Love You"?* Downers Grove, Ill.: InterVarsity, 1977. This book explains how husbands and wives can understand each other's expressions of love.

Swindoll, Charles. *Strike the Original Match.* Wheaton, Ill.: Living Books/Tyndale, 1980. Help for couples who need to renew the romance and joy in their marriage.

Talley, Jim. *Reconcilable Differences: Healing for Troubled Marriages.* Nashville: Thomas Nelson, 1990. Most couples who split quit too soon. Focusing on marriage and forgiveness, this book shows couples how to allow God's healing to ease hard times. It maintains that God wants relationships to work out—even in the event of divorce.

Wheat, Ed, and Gaye Wheat. *Intended for Pleasure.* Old Tappan, N.J.: Fleming H. Revell, 1961. Sexual techniques and sexual fulfillment in Christian marriage.

Wheat, Ed, and Gloria Okes Perkins. *Love Life for Every Married Couple.* Grand Rapids, Mich.: Zondervan, 1980. Provides practical insight on couples' conflicts, frustration, and unhappiness in their love life and offers ways to refresh or build a loving marital relationship.

Wyse, Lois. *Poems for the Very Married.* New York: Doubleday. Delightful poems that could only have been written to and by "the very married."

Yorkey, Mike, ed. *Growing a Healthy Marriage.* Colorado Springs: Focus on the Family, 1993. Help your marriage be all it can be.

Young, Ed. *Romancing the Home.* Nashville: Broadman, 1993. Dr. Young outlines God's design for marriage and suggests ways husbands and wives can contribute to the satisfaction and fulfillment of their spouses' needs.

Zoepfel, Glenn. *He Wins, She Wins.* Nashville: Thomas Nelson, 1994. How to stop the emotional tug of war that can destroy your marriage.

Magazines and Periodicals for the Christian Family

Adults

A Better Tomorrow, P.O. Box 50449, Boulder, Colorado 80321-0449. (Published by Publishing Directions, Inc., Thomas Nelson.) For senior citizens with a future.

Better Life, P.O. Box 50473, Boulder, Colorado 80995. (Published by Thomas Nelson.) Focuses on spiritual, physical, and emotional health for all ages.

Charisma and Christian Life, 600 Rinehart Road, Lake Mary, Florida 32746. This is an inspiring magazine for the charismatic Christian community.

Christian Parenting Today, P.O. Box 545, Mount Morris, Illinois 61054. The Christian magazine that offers practical and biblical advice for parents.

Christian Single, 127 Ninth Avenue North, Nashville, Tennessee 37234. This magazine is for never-marrieds and formerly-married adults.

Dads Only/Dads & Moms, Box 270616, San Diego, California 92198. This is a bi-monthly fathering and parenting newsletter.

Focus on the Family, Colorado Springs, Colorado 80995. This four-color magazine for families is available free from Focus on the Family.

Focus on the Family Newsletter, Colorado Springs, Colorado 80995. Written by Dr. James Dobson, this publication addresses timely issues of interest to the family.

Moody Magazine, 820 N. LaSalle Drive, Chicago, Illinois 60610. A magazine for the entire family, with provocative articles for adults and special sections for teenagers and children.

Parents of Teenagers, P.O. Box 545, Mount Morris, Illinois 61054. This Christian magazine offers parents of teens practical and biblical advice on navigating the difficult teenage years.

The Christian Reader, 465 Gundersen Drive, Carol Stream, Illinois 60188. This is a Christian *Reader's Digest*, with articles selected from many other periodicals and books.

The Single Parent Family, Colorado Springs, Colorado 80995. A magazine to encourage single parents.

Today's Christian Woman, 465 Gundersen Drive, Carol Stream, Illinois 60188. Whether you are single or married, a career woman or homemaker, *TCW* is for you, today's Christian woman.

Virtue, P.O. Box 545, Mount Morris, Illinois 61054. This magazine is for the woman who is serious about her faith, her marriage, and her family.

Washington Watch, Family Research Council, 700 Thirteenth St., N.W., Suite 500, Washington, D.C. 20005-3960. This newsletter briefly reports on news from our nation's capital regarding issues that affect the family.

Young People

Breakaway, Colorado Springs, Colorado 80995. This magazine encourages teen boys and gives them sound advice on how to handle the challenges of being a teenager.

Brio, Colorado Springs, Colorado 80995. This magazine encourages teen girls and gives them sound advice on how to handle the challenges of being a teenager.

Campus Life, P.O. Box 11618, Des Moines, Iowa 50340. Helps high school and early college students navigate adolescence with their faith intact.

Contemporary Christian Music, P.O. Box 5596, Boulder, Colorado 80321-5996. For anyone interested in contemporary Christian music and recording artists. Contains information about new releases, top song and album charts, and interviews.

Group, Box 481, Loveland, Colorado 80537. A magazine full of articles and ideas for teenagers, youth, and quest groups.

His, InterVarsity Press, Urbana, Illinois. Published by InterVarsity Press, this is probably the best magazine available today for the thinking young person who is serious about being His. For college age and beyond.

Youth Walk, Walk Thru the Bible Devotionals, P.O. Box 476, Mount Morris, Illinois 61054-9900. This is a daily devotional for youth.

Children

Faith 'n Stuff, 16 E. 34th Street, New York, New York 10016. A magazine for kids seven through twelve years old that has games, word puzzles, seasonal pieces, and fiction.

Focus on the Family Clubhouse, Colorado Springs, Colorado 80995. This fun-filled magazine brings exciting stories, puzzles, and jokes to kids ages eight through twelve.

Focus on the Family Clubhouse Jr., Colorado Springs, Colorado 80995. This magazine for children ages seven and younger includes puzzles, games, and stories.

It's God's World, God's World Publications, Box 2330, Asheville, North Carolina 28802. For kindergarten through junior high, this distinctly Christian magazine includes articles on history, the arts, politics, science, and human relations.

Audio and Video Products for Making Memories

The following audio and video resources are from Focus on the Family, Colorado Springs, Colorado 80995.

Audio

Adventures in Odyssey. Each six-cassette audio series contains twelve episodes and is packaged in a sturdy case. Designed for children ages five through twelve, these are stories from the radio drama series "Adventures in Odyssey."

Video

Adventures in Odyssey. An animated adventure series for children ages four through twelve.

McGee and Me. A dramatic series for older children and adults featuring Nick and his animated sidekick, McGee.

Blue, Ron. *Common Cents: Training Your Children to Manage Money.* Ron Blue introduces basic principles about money and a system for teaching your children about finances.

Demoss, Bob. *Learn to Discern.* Bob DeMoss addresses the media influence on young people and offers solutions to the media assault.

Adkins, Mike. *A Man Called Norman.* This is a dynamic story of two men who triumph over their fears to forge an uncommon friendship.

Doud, Guy. *Molder of Dreams.* America's National Teacher of the Year tells how to shape another's dreams and stresses the importance of family and Christian principles.

Sex, Lies, and . . . the Truth. This video contradicts the so-called "safe sex" message in a way that allows teens to draw their own conclusion that abstinence is the best option.

Other Special Products for Making and Keeping Memories

A red "You're Something Special" plate, handmade of fine ceramic. No two are exactly alike. See page 87 for ideas of how to use this plate to say "we love you" at special times. To order write to: The Original Red Plate Company, P.O. Box 7965, Newport Beach, California 92660.

Grandpa's Story or Grandma's Story, published by Wincroft Inc., Winona, Minnesota. This keepsake and memories album for grandchildren is made for grandmas and grandpas to record all kinds of details about themselves and their lives, the interests and hobbies they enjoyed, the kinds of childhoods they had, the places they lived, etc. The pages are actually envelopes in which grandparents can insert notes, letters, keepsakes, photographs, etc. This completed book makes a priceless gift for a grandchild. To order write to: Venture Management, 26 Ponco Trail, Kirkwood, Missouri 63122.